PENGUIN BOOKS

A Pictorial History of English Architecture

Photographs by

Julian Barnard

Ronald Clark

Margaret Harker

Birkin Haward

Michael Holford

Angelo Hornak

Dimitri Kasterine

A. F. Kersting

Hugh Lee

Edwin Smith

Jeremy Whitaker

Notes on the illustrations by

Nicholas Taylor

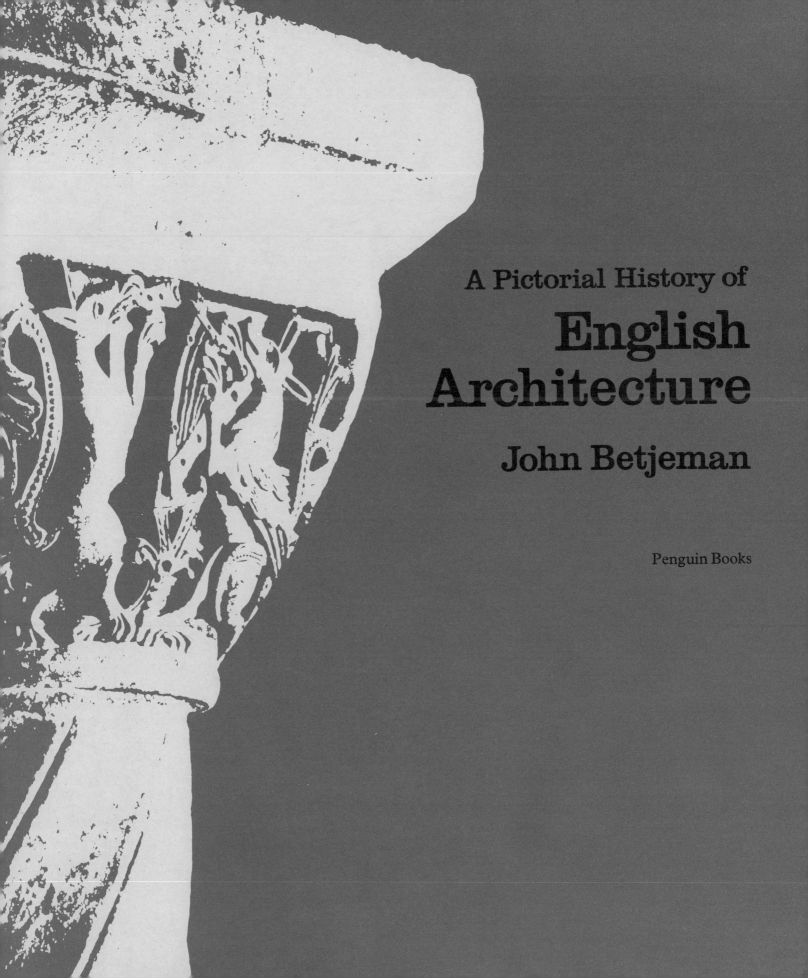

A Pictorial History of
English Architecture

John Betjeman

Penguin Books

Penguin Books Ltd, Harmondsworth,
Middlesex, England
Penguin Books Australia Ltd, Ringwood,
Victoria, Australia
Penguin Books Canada Ltd,
2801 John Street,
Markham, Ontario, Canada L3R 1B4
Penguin Books (N.Z.) Ltd,
182 - 190 Wairau Road,
Auckland 10, New Zealand

First published by John Murray 1972
Published in Penguin Books 1974
Reprinted 1977

This book was designed and produced
by George Rainbird Ltd,
36 Park Street, London W1Y 4DE
House Editor: Alison Cathie
Designer: Ronald Clark
Indexer: Myra Clark

Made and printed in Great Britain by
Impact Litho Ltd, Tolworth, Surrey
Set in Monophoto Plantin

To John G. Murray

Contents

Foreword

This book came into being in a way which will, I hope, prove to be fortunate. I was asked by the Editor of *The Daily Telegraph Magazine* to write twelve articles on English architecture. This meant that I had to think not just in terms of text but also of illustrations. I agree with the late F. E. Howard's dictum that one good photograph is worth ten pages of text. On the other hand the text had to be readable and without too many technical terms. Also the whole range of architecture had to be covered, and be proportioned. One has the impression at the back of one's mind that architecture stopped at the 18th century. This is a hangover from the Gothic Revival. Yet I hope I have been fair to all periods, for it is impossible to judge the present – we are of it. And he is brave, but not always wise, who thinks he knows what the architecture of the future is going to be and, by that standard, judges buildings being put up today.

There was not room to include Scotland, Ireland and Wales in this book. Each country has its distinctive style of architecture. Scottish architects and civil engineers have given much to English buildings and scenery. Ireland has given less; it had its own eminent architects and styles from the Romanesque to the late 19th century. John Nash (1752–1835), who transformed London, learned architecture in Wales. Scandinavia has left a magnificent medieval monument of her domination of the Northern Isles in the coloured sandstone cathedral of Kirkwall, Orkney.

I have always had so much pleasure from looking at buildings – a public art gallery which is always open – that I have wanted to convey my pleasure to others, even to those who don't read books on architecture: and small blame to them. The illustrations, at any rate, will, I hope, justify this book, though I must emphasize that a few of the illustrations of modern buildings at the end are here as cautionary examples – not because I admire them all. The succinct captions by Nicholas Taylor show why they were chosen.

A book should be a joy to handle and to look at. It need not be useful for passing exams. To communicate enthusiasm is what this book tries to do. It is bound to be personal. Its format has been made possible by John Hadfield, a pioneer of good modern book production, who is the editor of *The Saturday Book*, and by Ronald Clark and Alison Cathie.

If it encourages others to find excitement by using their eyes, and to stop and look at buildings, it will have been worth publishing.

JOHN BETJEMAN

The Beginnings and Saxon

THE EARLIEST ARCHITECTURE in Britain is standing stones and earthworks. Because these are prehistory, and the subject of the sometimes exciting science of archaeology, I was tempted to leave them out. There are the wrangles about dates, about the succession of prehistoric races which came to this island when the English Channel was narrower and easier to cross – the Neolithic people with long heads, the Bronze Age people with round heads, the wiry, Iron Age Celts, who were all here before the Romans landed.

They were hilltop peoples because the climate was damp and mild and the valleys were mostly forest and swamp and full of wild beasts. These peoples left behind earthworks and standing stones which we can see all over the downs and moors today. They cut figures into the sides of the chalk hills and they left in their mounded burial places urns, bones and trinkets from which we can deduce how they looked and what sort of decoration they favoured. From the rubbish heaps outside their fortlike cattle enclosures and the indentations in the ground which mark where they dwelt we can deduce what they ate, what sort of tools they used and how they lived.

They also left three monuments larger than any Saxon buildings and so impressive that they are part of our architectural history. Two of these are stone circles, Avebury and Stonehenge, both in Wiltshire. Even in the 17th and 18th centuries these stones were engraved on copper plates for antiquaries. By the time the Romantic movement had started their dumb and lonely mystery inspired Turner and Constable and many followers. Hardy recalls the effect of earthworks on the chalk downs in 'The Revisitation':

> Round about me bulged the barrows
> As before, in antique silence –
>   immemorial funeral piles –
> Where the sleek herds trampled daily
>   the remains of flint tipped arrows
> Mid the thyme and chamomiles . . .

The third great prehistoric monument is the triple ramparted earthwork of Maiden Castle in Dorset.

The earliest of these strange things, and much the biggest, is Avebury. In fact it is the largest megalithic monument in Europe and was started in about 1800 BC by Early Bronze Age people. It was an important religious centre like Mecca or Lourdes, and stone implements from North Wales and lava from the Rhine have been dug up in it. The enormous stone circle which comprises the temple contains two smaller circles and the whole structure is surrounded by an earth rampart.

These Early Bronze Age people knew the use neither of the wheel nor the horse.

OPPOSITE *Wrinkled and stretched like an elephant's skin, the sheep-cropped turf of the great Iron Age earthworks of Maiden Castle, Dorset, has a timeless quality which makes it hard for us to imagine the earth-moving without machinery that must have been involved; but the earthworks, even with their carefully guarded entrances, did not keep out the disciplined urban troops from Rome.*

ABOVE *Apparently constructed simultaneously with the first part of Stonehenge (c.1800 BC), Avebury is an amazingly extensive sequence of standing stones. From the 130-ft high artificial mound of Silbury, the so-called Kennet Avenue, a mile and a half long, leads to the main circular earthwork, inside which is a ring of stones – this big ring in turn enclosing two smaller rings. Within it all is the present-day village with its delightful Elizabethan manor house.*

Their chief tools were of stone, bone and wood. They broke up the ground with the antlers of deer and shovelled it into heaps with the shoulder-blades of oxen. They moved the stones – at Avebury these are of a type known as sarsen – by rolling them along on logs and lifting them up by means of wooden stakes and ropes made of hide.

No one knows what sort of worship went on in this temple. Judging by primitive forms of religion surviving in remote parts today, it was probably some form of worshipping spirits of good and evil who might be able to control the weather, ward off enemies and be propitiated by sacrifice. The rampart which surrounds Avebury has a ditch on the inside, instead of on the outside as it would have been in a fortified earthwork. This was to prevent the spirits from escaping into the open downs.

The stones are artificially shaped and of two sorts – oblong- and lozenge-shaped. The medieval village which has percolated into the enclosure with its thatched cottages and handsome church with Saxon remains seems quite modern by comparison with the temple in which it stands. Archaeologists have restored many of the standing stones which bigoted and frightened churchmen in the Middle Ages caused to be buried. Greedy farmers in the 17th and 18th centuries smashed up other stones and used them for building. Nevertheless Avebury is much more worth seeing now than it was 30 years ago. The trackways which lead to it, the avenue of standing stones, the surrounding prehistoric settlements and tombs and that mysterious man-made

Increasingly peaceful conditions after the Norman Conquest led to the creation of unfortified market towns, leaving earlier settlements on the hills stranded. In the case of Old Sarum, shown here in Constable's water-colour, the site was successively occupied as an Iron Age camp, a Roman city (Sorviodumun) and a Norman cathedral-cum-fortress. It was too short of water supplies to be a permanent medieval town. Of the castle only fragments survive and of the cathedral only foundations.

earthwork, Silbury Hill, make one realize that here was a civilization of European extent, known to have been peaceful and agricultural.

Stonehenge, more complete than Avebury, is slightly later and smaller. Its stones came from Wales and its situation – when there are no tourists about and one is not too aware of the ministrations of Government Departments in the form of railings and litter baskets – is as romantic as when it first inspired awe in the 18th century.

The Iron Age settlement of Maiden Castle, south-west of Dorchester, was also a fortress from which the Iron Age Celts dominated the earlier civilizations of this island. These Celts, who must have married the round-headed descendants of Bronze Age people, are what we mean by ancient Britons. They were the people Caesar saw and whom later Roman emperors tried to conquer.

I do not think that any of the relics of the three and a half centuries of Roman domination in Britain represent such complete architecture. Rome visibly survives in roads, street plans, the remains of villas with tessellated pavements, baths and ports. There are no mighty viaducts, arches and temples such as are found in France and Italy. The most impressive Roman relic is Hadrian's wall.

When the Romans left and the Celts stayed on we have what are called the Dark Ages of 400 and 500 AD. The Celts became Christians towards the end of the sixth century, when the Saxons came from what is now Germany and invaded this island. The Iron Age Celts looked down on them as smelly and savage and heathen into the bargain. But the Saxons were an adaptable people. Those in Kent were converted to Christianity in 597, and it is Saxon churches which are the first conscious and considerable architecture in England.

They were a river people and settled in the valleys, estuaries and marshes. The ending -ey and -ea to a place name is the Saxon word for an island in a marsh,

ABOVE *It is hard to see why Earls Barton church in Northamptonshire has so mighty a Saxon bell-tower, as apparently the church it served was quite tiny, the nave being the tower's ground floor. The little belfry windows as well as the larger first-floor openings are supported on the Saxon style of roll-moulded baluster column.*

OPPOSITE *There is a refreshing directness about Saxon sculpture even when, as in this Crucifixion at Daglingworth in the Gloucestershire Cotswolds, the actual technique is naive. The figures pose stiffly in the full frontal style of the Byzantine. Yet already there is the English concentration on the patterns of things – Longinus' spear and scourge, Stephaton's sponge and reed, the upward-flaring cross.*

BELOW *The biggest surviving 7th-century basilica north of the Alps is at Brixworth, Northamptonshire, its 140-ft length rhythmically unified by sturdy arches of re-used Roman brick. The long-demolished aisles were divided up into separate chambers called* porticus, *an early case of the Anglo-Saxon defiance of visual logic by practical convenience.*

e.g., Stepney, Chelsea. Some other signs of Saxon settlement are the endings -ham and -ton. They called the Iron Age Celts the Welsh and the place name Walton often means Welshtown.

The Celts seem to have settled down with them, though those who objected hung out in Wales, Cornwall, Scotland and Ireland, and have continued to feel different until today.

Yet the more one thinks about the Saxons the more one admires them. They divided our country into hundreds and shires. They reformed our laws, gave birth to our literature and started systematic education. Manors and parishes are a Saxon invention, and from their form of government, the folkmoot, our parliamentary system originated. They were beautiful artists on vellum and in metalwork, true poets and highly civilized. Almost all their kings were good and Alfred the Great (871–99), who for some strange reason has never been canonized, was mighty both in peace and war. Anglo-Saxon England became the most important influence in western Christendom. The Normans, who were the allies and kinsmen of the Vikings – the Saxons' great enemy – were coarse by comparison.

If it was only their buildings which survive we would not have very much by which to judge the quality of Saxon architecture and art. Fortunately their drawings and manuscripts remain, of which the Lindisfarne Gospels in the British Museum are famous among the first and most splendid of illuminated manuscripts in Western Europe. They belong to the 7th century and were the product of Saxon and Celtic artists, earlier and more elaborate than the *Book of Kells*. In fact, what has come to be known as Irish Romanesque decoration has Saxon art in its origins.

They were used to building in wood, which is why none of their houses remain; but the boundary ditches sometimes survive as sunken lanes. Saxon churches were, according to Hugh Braun, an attempt to create in wood the cruciform Byzantine plan. Instead of a central

dome there was the central spirelet. The sole extraordinary survival of Saxon wood building is the little church of Greensted, near Ongar, in Essex. It is much restored but has walls of split oak logs set vertically.

The Saxons became excellent workers in stone and made a cement which bonded the walls of their churches together better than the Normans were able to bond their walls. They used this cement for floors.

The walls of their churches are thin and strong, and the proportions lofty and impressive. Brixworth Church in Northamptonshire (c.670–90) is the largest building of its date north of the Alps. One really has to see Saxon churches inside to realize how different they are in scale and proportion from later churches.

It used to be thought that the Normans destroyed all Saxon buildings, but this is not so. Many perished because they were of wood. The Normans only pulled down the larger Saxon monastic buildings, and this they did for prestige reasons. Otherwise they contented themselves with adding aisles and heightening towers.

There are now known to be 238 churches in England which have traces of Anglo-Saxon origin. In the North Country the best preserved is Escomb in County Durham (c.700) and here one can get the impression of an early Saxon church. The interior was dark, the window openings high up, there was no glass and light filtered through fretted stone. The walls were no doubt covered with painted decoration and gold and silver and ironwork must have been used in some of the furnishings.

The best-preserved Saxon church to survive in the south is the early 10th-century one at Bradford-on-Avon in Wiltshire. This has been spared to us, carved angels and all, because it was long used as a barn and not recognized as a church – or the 'restorers' would have got at it. It stands near the medieval parish church of that delightful wool town. Other famous Saxon churches are Deerhurst, in Gloucestershire, Jarrow, in

Durham, Breamore, in Hampshire, Worth, in Sussex, Wing, in Buckinghamshire, Bradwell, in Essex, and Reculver, in Kent.

The strangely striking towers of the 10th century at Barnack and Earls Barton, in Northamptonshire, and Barton-on-Humber, in Lincolnshire, are decorated with smooth strips of stone which are an imitation of timber construction, though they perform no structural function. Some of the most moving Saxon work is in stone carving, as on the 7th-century cross at Bewcastle, Cumberland, and the 11th-century roods and crucifixions in Romsey Abbey, in Hampshire, and Langford, in Oxfordshire. The Saxons show how important proportion and care over detail may be.

My own favourite Saxon interior is the crypt under Repton Church in Derbyshire. It was started in the 8th century before the Danes invaded and were suppressed by King Alfred in 866. It was finished in the early 11th century with columns and vaulting. Although it is very small it gives an impression of size and great space as though its designers had captured holy air and encased it in stone.

OPPOSITE *The Saxons brought with them from the North German forests an instinct for building in timber, but the only one of their log churches to survive is Greensted-juxta-Ongar in Essex, dated recently by dendro-magnetic tests to about 850. The trunks are split vertically in halves to provide a smooth internal face.*

ABOVE *The chapel of St Laurence at Bradford-on-Avon, Wiltshire, is an almost perfect small Saxon church, long disused. The tall narrow proportions are characteristic, particularly the attenuated arches inside, and so is the surface patterning of arches devoid of structural meaning.*

BELOW *The architectural influence of Rome derived less from the military conquest of the Empire than from the missionary conquest of the Church after AD 597. St Cedd symbolically planted his little chapel of St Peter at Bradwell-on-Sea, Essex, on the footings of the outer wall of a great Roman fort.*

Norman

WHETHER IT IS THE RESULT of propaganda in old history books or not I do not know, but most people have the impression that when William the Conqueror arrived he brought civilization and fine stone buildings to a benighted people.

This is not quite true. The Saxons were a peaceful agricultural people when the Normans came in 1066. They were much finer artists than the Normans and they were better builders. At any rate they were better builders than were the first Normans to arrive.

The Saxons built in the round-arched style known as Romanesque because it was the style used throughout Christendom. It was meant to look like the round-arched architecture of ancient Rome. Romanesque is generally called 'Norman' in England, but quite a lot of what we think is Norman may possibly be Saxon. What must have happened was that, as the comparatively few Normans and the many native Saxons and Celts settled down, the Saxon gift for stone carving and masonry was used in buildings, so that one would be hard put to it to say who was a Saxon carver or who was a Norman one. The very imaginative carving on the church at Kilpeck in Herefordshire was done with a chisel, probably by Saxons. The more regular and mechanical-looking carving that one sees in East Anglia and in Kent, with the zig-zag moulding that is characteristic of early Norman, was done with an axe, probably by Normans.

The Normans drove the chief men of the Saxons out of the big houses and took over their land. William the Conqueror, who could neither read nor write, was what is today much admired – 'an able administrator'. Part of that administration, for which the Norman kings seem to have had a gift, was Domesday Book, which is the only guide we have to what Saxon and early Norman England was like. It survived because it was written on skin. Had paper been invented, we would never have seen it, as paper would not have lasted so long.

The total population of England in the 11th century is unlikely to have been more than one and a half million. When William the Conqueror arrived by far the biggest city was, as it still is, London. It then had only 10,000 inhabitants.

Houses were built of wood. The only exceptions were those which belonged to the very important, and those in stone districts on the limestone belt which stretches from Yorkshire down to Somerset and Dorset. Alfred the Great's palace had been a wooden building.

Villages must have looked rather like the primitive settlements you see in missionary magazine photographs – that is to say they were clearings in the forest or islets in the marsh or a little shaved part of the moor and scrub; and in this clearing there would have been a large house of wood and the other large timber building would have been the church; and there would have been a series of modest hovels made of branches leant against one another, and walled between the branches with mud and roofed with thatched grass or turf. Smoke came out of a hole in the middle of the roof from a fire in the middle of the floor, as I have seen it coming out of a 'black' house in Foula, the westernmost of the Shetland Islands.

ABOVE *The far-ranging Normans were able to loot traditional cultures all the way from Northern Europe to Jerusalem, and even in the Herefordshire countryside the village church of Kilpeck (c.1140) displays a bewildering internationalism in its sculpture. Influences range from Burgundian to North Italian in the figures to the Viking Ringerike style and Celtic manuscripts in the vivaciously interlaced dragons.*

OPPOSITE *The nave of Waltham Abbey, its groove-patterned piers arranged in pairs on the model of Durham, is characteristic of the usual three-storey Norman elevation. The gallery over the aisles has arched openings almost as tall as those of the main arcade. But even the scalloped capitals and zig-zag arches are outfaced by the incredibly exuberant east wall, designed in 1860 by the Victorian romantic William Burges, and glowing with Burne-Jones glass.*

These primitive houses were arranged either along each side of a confluence of roads or round a green, and the track to the next settlement might have been through forest or wild country. Behind the houses stretched fields which were cultivated by a communal rota system; in the street in front and beyond the open drains was the market place. To this day one can get a faint idea of the traditional growth of a town if one goes into a small country town which has as yet been spared development. Very often the houses in the High Street still have long gardens stretching out behind them and into the open fields. And the open fields in Saxon times would have been called out-fields, and beyond them would have been forests.

In some country towns you can still see fields and trees at the end of the roads from a market hall which stands on stilts where the roads meet. I should not think any of the wooden houses survive from Norman times, although in districts where half-timber construction is the traditional style of architecture, as in Worcestershire, East Anglia, Kent and Sussex, some older cottages follow the principles that the Saxons and Normans used for timber houses. In a stone district, a perfect example of a medieval (actually Norman) town house is the building known as the Jew's House in Lincoln.

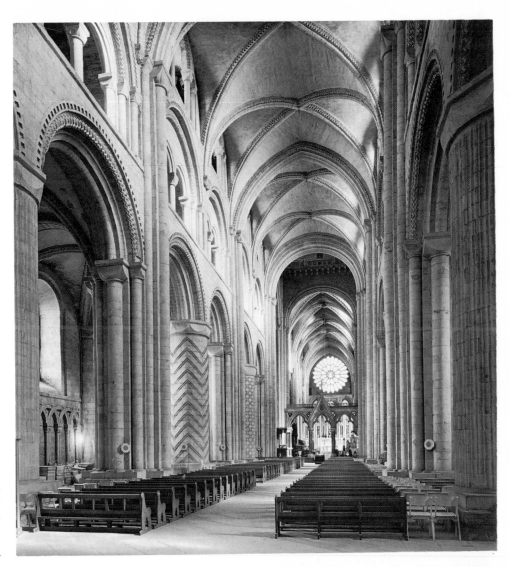

OPPOSITE *The greatest of the Norman fortified keeps was naturally the king's own White Tower in London, completed in 1097 under the soldier-bishop Gundulph of Rochester. Within it at second-floor level is secreted the Chapel of St John, a complete church with a perfectly preserved sequence of arcades and ambulatories round a tunnel-vaulted apse.*

ABOVE *The mighty piers of Durham Cathedral with their deep-cut patterns of spirals, lozenges and fluting support Europe's first high-rib vault (begun 1093). Already the transverse arches are pointed, foreshadowing the Gothic. This began the process of concentrating the weight of buildings on specific points, thus releasing the wall surfaces for the heavenly mysteries of stained glass.*

BELOW *Barely 50 ft long and as richly wrought as an ivory casket, Barfreston church flexes its muscles on a smooth grass hillock near Dover. The elaborate portal shows the English passion for patterning again, its modest-sized Christ enmeshed in loops of foliage, with signs of the zodiac and labours of the months on the outer arches.*

The first buildings the Normans erected in England were castles set at strategic points. Many of these were of wood. The best preserved stone one is Castle Hedingham, in Essex. The most famous is the White Tower in London. The castles, whether they were of stone or wood, were where the Norman barons lived, and with the aid of knights and retainers kept the Saxons and Iron Age Celts in subjection.

The Saxon parish system already existed and was taken on by the Normans. They rebuilt many of the wooden churches, and that is why so many parish churches in England have Norman remains in them. But chiefly the Normans encouraged monks and nuns to come over and settle – the Benedictines first and then the Cistercians. With Caen stone floated over from France they started to rebuild Canterbury, the centre of southern English Christianity. Most of the medieval cathedrals of England were Norman in origin and so were many other fine abbeys which have never become cathedrals, such as Malmesbury, Tewkesbury and Romsey in the South and Selby and Cartmel in the North.

Monasteries were the refuges of learning and devotion – which is one reason why the abbeys are such a prominent part of the Romanesque architecture of England. Nature loomed larger than man. Human life was cheaper. If you were in the forests an enemy might be hiding waiting to kill – an Anglo-Saxon if you were a Norman, a Norman if you were an Anglo-Saxon, a Celt if you were either. In addition to fear from man, there was a fear of wild animals, of being lost, of ghosts, and there were many terrifying survivals of paganism.

That remarkable writer John Harvey, in his book *English Cathedrals*, gives a memorable description of the spirit in which Norman architecture was built in Britain:

> The dark world of outer barbarism was still present in men's minds. Not until the fresh knowledge and the new Gothic spirit swept Europe in the succeeding century were men to feel that they lived in a bright and open

world. The sombre gloom of cave-dwelling and cave-worship hangs over the monk's choir of St Albans, the long nave of Peterborough; flickers like a grey shadow glimpsed from the corner of an eye in the transept of Winchester. Dark enough now, but with the opacity of early glass midnight must have reigned at noon.

These Norman churches had very small windows high up; only the most important abbey churches, like Canterbury, could afford stained glass. Other buildings had stone grilles perforated for the light to come through, or there may have been linen soaked in oil to let in the light and keep out the weather. The monks said their offices behind high screens, and you can see that arrangement surviving in St Albans Abbey today.

The abbeys were constructed with very thick walls, but the Norman builders were not so skilled at laying foundations as the

OPPOSITE *The Normans as warriors devised the fortified tower keep, set within encircling earthworks and palisades, as peculiarly their own ideal of the high life for noblemen. Castle Hedingham in Essex, splendidly sheer from without, has staircases and small chambers scooped out of the thickness of the main walls.*

ABOVE *In view of the Church's outlawing of usury among Christians, the financing of trade naturally devolved upon the Jews. At Lincoln, where Henry II forcibly seized vast sums from Aaron the Jew, there are two well-preserved merchant's houses of the late 12th century, both known as the Jew's House. The main hall was on the upper floor.*

MIDDLE *The gradual lightening of the Norman style after the invention of the rib vault is illustrated at Durham in the so-called Galilee or Lady Chapel added to the west front of the cathedral (c.1190). Although the arches are still ornamented with zig-zag, they are carried on slender shafts of Purbeck marble from Dorset.*

BELOW *The hall of Oakham Castle, Rutland, pinpoints functionally as well as visually the coming of age of English domestic architecture. It was not really a castle, but a fortified manor house, establishing for the first time the conventional grouping of three doorways at the entrance or 'screens passage' end, leading to kitchen, pantry and buttery. The round-headed arches, slim and elegant, are already decorated with the dogtooth ornament of Gothic, while the aisle window frames actually have pointed heads.*

Saxons had been. They used to build cross-shaped buildings with central towers designed to dominate the district and increase the prestige both of the Church and the Normans. Many of these central towers collapsed because of faulty foundations. Indeed, the fall of the central tower at Ely resulted in that splendid lantern being put in its place later in the Middle Ages.

The walls of the Norman churches were painted inside – generally brownish, with red lines in squares and patterns. Where the light fell on an inside wall coloured figures of saints and angels might be painted, and an attempt was probably made at the east end to give the effect of the mosaics of an Eastern basilica. Several examples of Norman painting survive, the most perfect probably being that of St Paul in St Anselm's Chapel in Canterbury Cathedral.

To begin with, Norman churches and abbeys were generally round-ended at the east – that is to say, apsidal. The nearer to France the more there were these round ends. But the Celts in England liked a square east end where the altar is. As time went on round-ended churches were squared off at the east end, and sometimes they were built, even in Norman times, with a square end.

The Norman churches of England, whether they are cathedral churches or parish churches, but particularly the cathedral churches, differ from those on the Continent in their variety and in their size. In England they are longer and larger than in France, particularly the cathedrals, but they are not so tall.

Different parts of the country have different styles of Romanesque. In the naves at Gloucester and Tewkesbury there is a very distinctive West Country Romanesque style – immensely thick cylindrical columns and rather small round arches on top of them. At Peterborough, a late Norman building, the columns in that splendid nave are very tall. The most perfect of all the Norman buildings of England is undoubtedly Durham Cathedral. Here the columns have zig-zag patterns and other designs incised on them, rather as though they were painted in that dark red paint the Normans liked to use. At the west end of Durham there is the Galilee porch which is in a late Romanesque style, and unique in England.

We all of us have our favourite Norman buildings. Durham comes first with me, but for mystery and a sense of endlessness I cannot make up my mind whether I prefer the crypt at Worcester Cathedral, with its cushion capitals and many vistas, or that under Canterbury Cathedral, which is part of an early Norman building where Becket must have walked.

ABOVE *The nave of St Albans Cathedral (built 1077–88) is the place for experiencing the overwhelming massiveness desired by the conquering Normans. Arches are cut into walls as into solid rock, without the individual support of columns or shafts, the cave-like effect enhanced by the undulating surfaces of stucco. The mural paintings by contrast, each of them originally above a side altar, show 13th-century humanism at its best.*

OPPOSITE *The stained glass of the choir of Canterbury Cathedral is as good as any in France – not only the vividly pictorial medallions of Thomas Becket's life in the main ambulatory windows (made c.1220), but also the earlier series in the clerestory, probably of c.1180, depicting the Old Testament ancestors of Christ. This one is now in the west window of the late 14th-century nave.*

Early English

HIGHER THAN THE FOREST TREES, nobler than the baron's castles, the English monasteries of the 13th century soared heavenward in stone. They were the beginning of a national style. We call it Early English and it grew out of the round-arched Norman style.

The names for the architectural styles of medieval England were devised by a Quaker architect, Thomas Rickman, in 1817, and they have stuck. He called Romanesque Norman. The style which might be called Early Pointed, when people were just beginning to find out about the pointed arch, he called Transitional. This was followed by Early English, Decorated and Perpendicular. Each style lasted roughly a century. The Early English lasted from 1150 to 1250, that is to say through the reigns of Henry II, Richard I, John and Henry III, a period when the King and the barons were less powerful than the Church, and when England was still closely connected with Northern France.

Churches were therefore the most prominent buildings. They rose, many steepled, out of walled cities. Lincoln must have looked superb on its hill when the three towers of its cathedral were finally completed with spires in the 14th century. The west front of Wells (1240) was a sculpture gallery of outdoor figures ranged in long rows in niches. The whole of this west front of Wells was painted in many colours, so that it must have seemed as startling as an oriental temple would today if it were standing over the Somerset meadows.

The Early English style usually has acutely pointed arches, slender columns, sometimes clustered together like pipes of stone, and, on the top of the columns, capitals, very often carved with leaves and forming a bell shape. The mouldings of the arches are deep and you can put your hand right into them. Salisbury, Lincoln, Wells and Worcester are cathedrals which are outstanding examples of the Early English style, though many other cathedrals exhibit it. Parish churches are sometimes in the Early English style. For instance, one of the finest is West Walton in Norfolk, and another is Abbey Dore in Herefordshire. A third is Uffington in Berkshire.

Where a parish church has Early English features, whether it be a chancel window or an arcade, you can generally be

OPPOSITE *The masons at Lincoln Minster combined the most elaborate illusions of structure, in the classic form of Purbeck marble shafting, with the most unexpected irregularities of pace and rhythm throughout the eighty-eight years' rebuilding (1192–1280). The vault in the south aisle, for example, breaks up the continuity of its ridge-rib between each bay. Capitals and corbels throughout have the exquisite formalized foliage known as stiff-leaf.*

BELOW *Wells west front exhibits the curious English unconcern with establishing a logical relationship between the grand façade and the structure that lies behind it. Instead of the systematic French hierarchy of portals and windows, strictly one to each aisle, Bishop Jocelyn's master mason at Wells draped indiscriminately across them a myriad array of Biblical statuary like a giant tapestry. The towers were not completed until c.1400.*

certain that the church was connected with an abbey which supplied its priests and caused it to be built. Sometimes a rich abbey would build, even bigger than the church, a barn in the district, where it collected its tithes from the farmers. The Abbey of Beaulieu, in Hampshire, built the great stone barn of Great Coxwell in Berkshire in the 13th century. The monasteries and convents were really the equivalent of large industries today: they drew people to them and they supplied work.

When we are told in the guide book that Bishop So and So built this or that part of a cathedral or a church, it was not he who did the work of building but the master mason. John Harvey, the architectural writer, has found out the names of many of these medieval masons. They moved from job to job and their styles can be recognized. Nothing is known about them personally. We shall not know what, in about 1200, gave the designer of the famed west front of Peterborough Cathedral the brilliant idea of making the central of his three great arches smaller than those which flank it. At the time the custom had been to reverse that arrangement – a large arch in the middle and smaller ones at the sides.

Medieval men were smaller in stature than we are today. They lived in squalid wooden cottages with earth floors in front of clearings in the forest. These were their villages, and they stayed in the monasteries very often when they worked for the monks on the building of the abbeys. That they should have produced such splendid and complete buildings as Salisbury and Lincoln and Wells and Worcester in the Early English style is a source of wonder. There are various reasons. Firstly it was an age of great faith and building was a pleasure and there were fewer distractions than now. And secondly the Church must have been a calmer and more regular taskmaster than the hunting barons, who had gone off on Crusades against the infidels.

The most rational explanation of the origin of Early English Gothic and therefore of the Gothic style generally, the style

ABOVE *The Herefordshire church of Abbey Dore shows the gradual evolution from the still-massive transitional Norman to the multi-facetted shafting of Early English, paralleling at the same time a shift in the Cistercian Order towards greater luxury. The choir was extended and then opened up through three noble arches to the diagonal vistas of the vaulted double ambulatory.*

OPPOSITE *Peter de Wint's painting of Lincoln Minster with the 14th-century Pottergate in the foreground captures the misty atmosphere of the hilltop precinct. Lincoln codified the characteristic proportions of the English cathedral, long and broad and low, where the French would be short and narrow and high. But the English have always compensated by erecting high towers – in the case of Lincoln originally with spires as well.*

BELOW *The classical intellects of the 13th century, the founders of universities, have their counterpart even in military architecture. Within the Norman shell keep of Restormel Castle, Cornwall, Henry III's brother used his profits from the local lead mines to create a geometrical ring of state rooms round a circular courtyard.*

of the pointed arch, is the necessity to roof an oblong space with stone. Wooden roofs were always catching alight. Chartres Cathedral was burned in 1020, Vézelay in 1120. In 1174, four years after the murder of Becket, the newly completed choir of Canterbury was burned to the ground amid the groans of the monks, who cursed God and their patron saints for allowing such a thing to happen.

William of Sens was the architect called from France to rebuild the choir of Canterbury in 1175. For three years it was rebuilding and he re-roofed it in stone in the French way. He was roofing in what is called sexpartite vaulting, that is to say he was using a pointed arch instead of a round arch. This had already been attempted over the choir of Durham Cathedral.

The Normans knew about vaulting a square space. They used the old Roman method of quadripartite vaulting, that is to say two stone half cylinders of equal height crossing one another at right angles. When you have to vault an oblong space in stone obviously one pair of arches is going to be larger than the other pair, therefore the only thing to do is to pinch up the smaller pair until it is as high as the larger pair. This brings about the pointed arch. The vaulting is thus divided into six and the compartments are separated by stone ribs.

At Durham you can see this crudely attempted; the point is there and the detail still takes one back to the old days of the Romanesque. In Canterbury you still have a sense of France and the Romanesque in the columns of the choir; but the vaulting above, with the thin ribs of stone, is without a hint of the Romanesque style about it. If you want to see what the roofs of Norman churches were like when they were of wood and before the stone vaulting of oblong spaces had been discovered, then Peterborough Cathedral nave has the largest painted Romanesque wooden roof in Europe. The Early English style of the pointed stone vaulting of a nave carried to perfection is to be found at Salisbury and Wells – and best of all at Lincoln.

These three cathedrals are very much in the English style, and are not like the choir of Canterbury, which is distinctly French.

A way of vaulting an oblong space which was much used on the Continent in Romanesque days was to create a barrel vault, that is to say one long half cylinder of stone running down the whole length of the nave as a roof. But, of course, such a roof exerted very strong outward pressure on the walls, as did the steep-pitched

ABOVE *When Laurence of Ludlow acquired the small Norman castle of Stokesay, he kept one small tower, and added to it a lofty great hall, with big windows of bar tracery as freely and openly exposed to arrows over the moat as to the protected courtyard. The gateway, on the left in this picture, shows typical West Midlands Elizabethan half-timber work over an earlier ground floor.*

MIDDLE *The Angel Choir of Lincoln (consecrated 1280) takes its name from the thirty angels in the spandrels of the arcade. Yet even here the flowers and leaves are dominant – oak, vine, maple, ranunculus and water lily, carved now with the complete naturalism familiar from St Francis' Canticle of the Sun. Following the introduction from France, via Westminster Abbey, of bar tracery, the clerestory windows show in the separate surfaces of their double tracery the dissolution of the solid wall into a many-coloured translucence symbolic of Heaven.*

BELOW *The nave and transepts of Wells Cathedral, the other canonical work of Early English Gothic besides Lincoln, have their restrained serenity of horizontal stress enlivened on a miniature scale by the luxuriantly carved stiff leaf capitals. Popping out from under the tufts of foliage and chasing round the multiple projections and recessions of the clustered shafts, twenty-four to each pier, is a strip cartoon of comic characters, including the apple stealer who robs an orchard but is then caught by a farmer with a pitchfork.*

OPPOSITE *The great hall of Stokesay was evidently remodelled internally in the 15th century, for against its end is the evidence, in silhouetted timbers, of an original layout of nave and aisles, with a row of posts on each side. The staircase to the upper floor of the Norman north tower was originally separated from the main body of the hall by the screens passage, which at ground level formed an internal draught lobby to the main entrance. The graceful proportions and generous lighting from broad windows are characteristic of the opening up of the medieval spirit to the fresh air of the outside world.*

wooden roofs of earlier churches and halls. However, as soon as you point the arches and distribute the thrust of the stone at certain points along the wall, instead of all along the wall, you can have much thinner walls between large buttresses which counteract the thrust of the stone vaulting. Thus the walls of the new churches like Lincoln Cathedral, Salisbury Cathedral and Wells have large buttresses along them; but between the buttresses the walls can be fairly thin.

Even in Norman times, before they discovered pointed arches for stone vaulting, they had been enlarging the little windows high up into large round-headed windows. Now that they had discovered that walls could be thinner they also enlarged the windows. In fact every monastery and every parish church that could afford it wanted to rebuild in the new pointed style.

Monasteries and churches – with the single exception of Salisbury, which was all built in the 13th century, except for its spire, which is a century later – are the gradual growths of centuries and they are built in the form of addition upon addition. The new pointed style could rise higher than the Romanesque churches and the buildings could be broader. As it was extremely important that the services

LEFT *It is ironical that Westminster Abbey, the crowning place of England's kings, should be so thoroughly un-English in design: French in its exaggerated height in proportion to breadth, French in its polygonal apse and chevet of radiating chapels, French in its bar tracery derived from Rheims. Henry III's mason when work started in 1245 was Henry of Reyns; no doubt it was when the Englishman John of Gloucester took over in 1253–4 that certain English features intruded higher up, for example the ridge-rib of the vault with its countervailing stress on the horizontal.*

OPPOSITE *William Morris called Great Coxwell tithe barn 'as noble as a cathedral', thus in a sense acknowledging that this vast 13th-century emporium below the Berkshire Downs, which brought in revenue for the Cistercian monks of Beaulieu, was just as authentic an expression of medieval ambition as the great churches themselves. Stone buttresses and walls enclose an interior entirely of timber, with nave and aisles divided by posts.*

should continue uninterrupted in the choirs of the cathedrals while the building was going on, the extensions were made round them. The fact is that they were always adding to them, particularly at the east end, where they had the shrines of the saints. This system of building additions all the time accounts for the great length of English cathedrals, and the way one aisle leads into another, and transept leads to chapel, and chapel gives a glimpse of yet another chapel.

The new style, Early English, was sculpture become architecture. It was as though the Saxons had been allowed to use their chisels and had ousted the rough axed surface decoration of the Normans. And as the style went on, carving abounded: carved capitals on the tops of columns, with leaves, or things that looked like leaves, springing from them. In fact, it was, in every sense of the word, the springtime of architecture. Great delight was taken by carvers of corbels and capitals in introducing little figures, peasants, listening monks, boys, bears, pigs, nuns, gossips.

The larger windows let in more light on to the carving. The pieces of glass leaded together in these large windows were still small and the prevailing colours, where figures were introduced, were blue, olive green, deep red and brownish pink for depicting human flesh, and very black outlines. There was much grisaille, that is to say silvery-grey glass, in the tall Early English windows. No Early English cathedrals or churches today have the complete decorative scheme that they had when they were built, though the Victorians made some gallant attempts to recreate them. We can only get an idea of what they looked like from fragments of painting on walls, and from glass, where it survives.

When Sir Gilbert Scott, the Victorian cathedral restorer, was working at Salisbury with his son George Gilbert Scott Junior, they found a lot of the colour in the nave and choir behind the whitewash with which the cathedral had been adorned inside. George Gilbert Scott Junior says:

The ruling intention appears to have been to have coloured window glass and richly coloured wall-spaces. The stained glass, of which a few fragments have escaped the vandalism of the Puritans and the stupidity of the chapter, was remarkable both by absence of figurework and the unusual predominance of white glass. The walls, on the contrary, were painted a full red, relieved by bold scroll work in black, and the mouldings were decorated upon the same system.

Thus the marble work, instead of showing, as it now does, almost black upon white, was designed to be in perfect tone, as regards chiaroscuro, with the red and the black of the wall-spaces. The only parts in which white was employed as a ground were the vaultings, the ribs of which were decorated in full colour, while the inter-spaces were occupied by medallions, in which red is again the predominating tint.

The red was of that brownish earth colour sometimes seen on the walls of old country churches.

A pilgrimage to a shrine in one of these new abbey churches must have been a startling series of experiences – the journey through the wild country, the resting at an inn provided by the monastery, the way out of the ordinary world marked by a great screen of stone images across the west front of the abbey, as at Wells and Salisbury and Lincoln. Then the pilgrim walked under this screen through a comparatively low door out of the light into unimaginable painted wonder, seen in the mitigated light of silvery glass. There were twinkling altars and statues everywhere, a sense of vista beyond vista, the monks screened off in their stalls chanting as one passed by on the way to the shrine of the saint, expecting a miracle and a blessing. There was an attempt in these Early English Gothic abbeys and churches to create a semblance of Heaven on earth, with their stone, colour, music and ritual. We go to foreign lands as the people of the Middle Ages went to cathedrals. And to them they must have seemed more impressive than our first sight of New York to us.

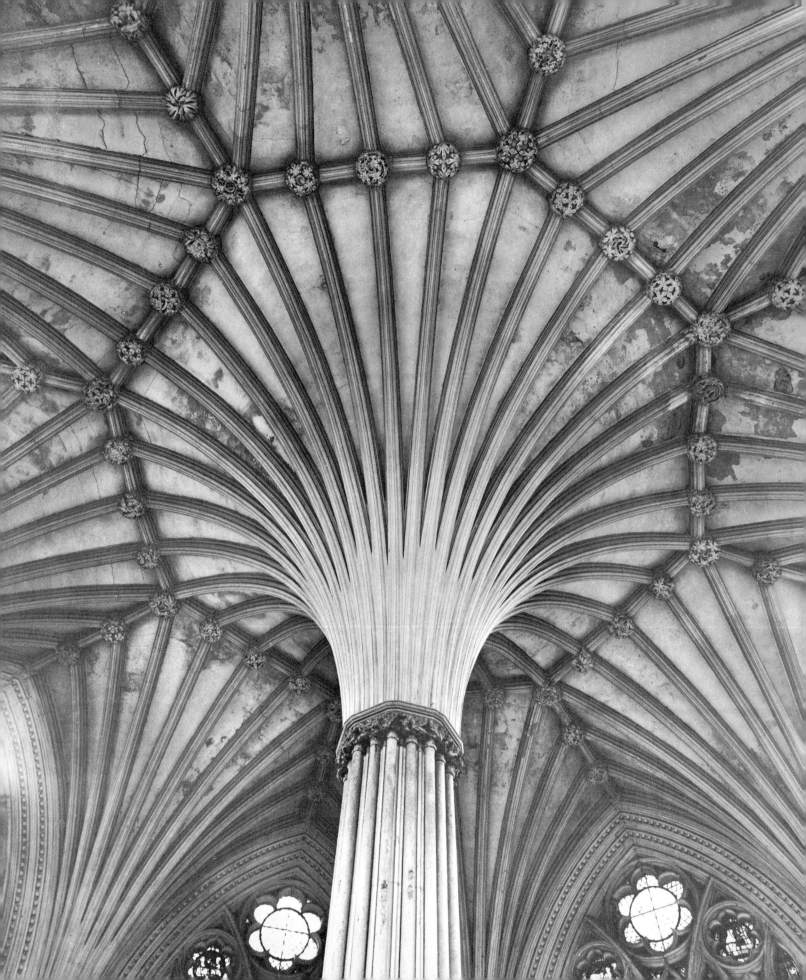

Decorated

THE PHRASE 'MERRY ENGLAND' begins to apply to this country when the Decorated period of architecture was born. You cannot call the round-arched Romanesque architecture of the Saxons and Normans merry. It was dark and prisonlike inside whether it was a hut, castle or church. Any jokes there were survive only in surface decoration and literature. The Early English style, with its aspirations to height and more light, is more ascetic and earnest than cheerful. It was popular with Cistercian monks who disapproved of much decoration and set great store by proportion, as at Fountains and Rievaulx Abbeys in Yorkshire. The Cistercians catered for the reforming, puritan part of everybody's make-up.

The Decorated style lasted roughly from 1272 to 1377, through the reigns of the three King Edwards. Castles had their drawbridges down for long periods, serfs were less cowed, knights were often chivalrous, farmers and weavers grew rich on wool and exported it abroad, landowners began to live in unfortified houses; a new class was starting which was not a baronial one but legal and mercantile.

Churches were still the most prominent buildings. Abbeys belonging to the monastic orders were waning in importance. Secular clergy – that is to say, priests gathered together in one place to serve a great church, but not under the rule of St Benedict or St Augustine, or any other of the orders – were growing in influence.

The cathedrals of Chichester, Exeter, Hereford, Lichfield, Lincoln, St Paul's, Ripon, Salisbury, Southwell, Wells and York were all served by secular canons.

They went in for chapter houses where they discussed business. Sometimes they built cloisters, as at Salisbury, though they did not really need them as did the monks of the Benedictine orders and Augustinian orders for contemplation and for doing their work when it was raining. They wanted to seem as important and holy as the monks. I daresay they were.

The stock description of the Decorated style for churches is true enough:

Arches equilateral; windows large and divided into two or more lights by mullions, the tracery in the head geometrical or flowing, diamond-shaped piers; capitals bell-shaped; bases generally formed of the quarter round and scroll moulding; rich doorways and windows, often surrounded with triangular or ogee canopies; mouldings bold and finely proportioned, the ball and four-leaved flower predominate; parapets pierced with quatrefoils and flowing tracery; niches, pinnacles, crosses etc., very chaste.

This all goes to show that the designers of churches were becoming more and more interested in structure, in letting in more light through windows between the buttresses of large churches, whose roofs were vaulted in stone, and in the smaller churches where the roofs were vaulted elaborately with wood. To support these large windows they introduced bars of stone called tracery, in richly varying patterns.

The earliest tracery was geometrical, as though done with compasses, and branched out later into flowing shapes like unfolding flower petals. The stained glass was held in position both by the

ABOVE *The weakness of Decorated is its substitution of licentious ornament for the noble discipline of Early English. Southwell Minster's chapter house, begun c.1290, is a peculiarly satisfying combination of the noble discipline of Early English, derived from Lincoln, with the new freedom of naturalistic ornament. Capitals, corbels and arches are encrusted with the leaves and flowers of the hop, the maple, the hawthorn, the oak and the vine.*

OPPOSITE *The 'palm tree' effect of the Wells Cathedral chapter house central pillar derives from the tierceron vaulting of the West Country masons at Exeter. Thirty-two ribs well up in a fountain of crisp-cut stone, hang in the air in a sprayed out circle of carved bosses, and then plunge downwards again to the clustered vaulting shafts between the windows.*

ABOVE *The nave of York Minster, begun c.1290, still contains almost all its original glass. This window, in the south aisle, of the martyrdom of St Andrew shows the increasingly wide range of lighter pot-metals that had become available, in place of the earlier concentration on deep reds and blues.*

OPPOSITE *The staircase to the chapter house of Wells dates from c.1270 but in its free-flowing space – given an extra twist by time's erosion of the treads into a wave-like unevenness – it looks forward to the radical experiments of the West Country masons a generation later. It is in fact the upspreading branch of the steps to the right which leads into the chapter house itself with a double veil of tracery across its entrance; the flight straight ahead leads onto the Chain Gate of c.1460, bridging across the Cathedral Green to the delectable courtyard of the Vicar's Close.*

RIGHT *Ely Lady Chapel is predictably Decorated where Ely Octagon is unpredictable. It is a single rectangular room, but it was originally transformed into a flickering mystery by stained glass and flowing tracery. The glass was bashed out by the Puritans, so the pleasure now lies lower down, in the delicious details of the arcaded seats along the walls, like those of a chapter house. Each seat is canopied with a 'nodding ogee' – an ogee arch curving three-dimensionally forward as well as sideways – the whole wall surface, however straight a line on plan, being made to sway and ripple without ceasing.*

The graceful femininity of the Decorated style found a natural expression in spires, as in the triple group at Lichfield Cathedral, which preserve their outlines all the sharper after much rebuilding following the Civil War. The west *front (begun c.1280) is now a gallery of Victorian piety, including a statue of the Queen amongst the saints. The Close has the usual English approach down cobbled alleyways into the peace of the grassed churchyard.*

stone tracery and by bars of iron. In colour the stained glass was mostly silvery white or olive green, dark yellow, blue and red, and it depicted saints, generally in full-length figures with borders round them.

The most famous stained glass of the Decorated period is a golden window at the east end of the choir of Wells Cathedral. The most beautiful walk through stained glass, that is to say through a whole passage of stained glass, is out of the north transept of York Minster into the chapter house.

The Decorated period was one of marvellously deep-cut naturalistic sculpture; oak leaves, hawthorn leaves, berries, vines and ivy leaves adorned arches and capitals to columns. The most famous of these are the doors to the chapter house at Southwell Minster, and in the chapter house itself. The arcading of the walls of the lady chapel at Ely Cathedral is described by Alec Clifton-Taylor as 'like a parsley bed'. In York, Lincoln and Lichfield there is equally elaborate stone carving, some of it full of people and mythical animals. The most carved of all Decorated cathedrals, outside and in, is the stately Lichfield, with its three red sandstone spires; the most splendid as interiors are Exeter Cathedral and the miniature cathedral at Ottery St Mary in Devon. The largest Decorated cathedral, and the one with the most stained glass, is York Minster.

All the stonework – except in places where the natural colours of the stone are used as decorative features, as in the counties of Northampton and Rutland, where brown ironstone contrasts with creamy white limestone – was painted externally and internally in bright colours.

A pilgrimage to a cathedral or an abbey or a large church was the one adventure of life in the Middle Ages. It was, as we have seen, the equivalent of foreign tours today. You went not in search of sun but of saints, whose relics you believed – and their monkish guardians delighted to tell you so – could, if you were truly penitent, perform a miracle, cure you of a disease, bring you to a good death, or earn you remission from sins when the time came for you to go to Purgatory.

This description of the religion of medieval England sounds as if it were one more of fear than of love. But this is not so. The luxuriant life of the forests – hunting hares and coneys – hammering craftsmen, laughing peasants and comic tales were carved in wood and stone on the stalls of the monks and round the arches of the churches. There is an amusing miserere, that is to say, the under-part of a monk's stall, in Sherborne Minster, where a boy is depicted being whipped by a schoolmaster. All these are carvings of the Decorated period, showing the cheerful and exuberant nature of the English race.

Pilgrims such as Chaucer describes generally entered their cathedral by way of the west door, and the west entrance itself was often a kind of coloured screen, a foretaste of the screen that you would see, when you got into the cathedral, sheltering the monks and the holy relics of the east end from the people's part, the nave of the church. Out of the wet or the sun, through the porch into the nave with its light coming through stained glass windows, its painted walls and the murmur of neighbours and strangers round about – that is where you would walk if you were a pilgrim.

You would walk through the wooden carved screen, or maybe the stone carved screen, out of the nave into the hushed holiness beside the choir, and then, in a building taller and more marvellous than any you had ever seen, you would finally come to a place where there was a crowd, and that was the shrine of the saint.

The relics might be exposed and it might be a feast day. And then, on your way back down the other aisle from the one by which you had entered, you would go by, looking at altars and tombs, walking into a transept and then finally back through the screen into the nave where there were more pilgrims coming in, until you went out into an England of forests,

chases and wooden houses and white-walled cities, and the glittering steeples on the stone towers of the many churches.

This was a time when parish churches started to emulate cathedrals. The richest man in the parish might wish to save his soul, and those of his ancestors and present family, by paying a priest to say mass for them in a special chapel with its own altar. This was called a chantry chapel. When he died the rich man of the parish would be buried under the canopied niche of stone in the side wall of his chantry chapel. Then the various trades of the village might wish to enlarge their church with a special altar for the trade guild, the cobblers or the weavers or the carpenters. Masons who had worked on

large abbey churches a generation before would be called on to help to enlarge the church. In this way, many splendid churches of the Decorated period were built.

Some of them looked like miniature cathedrals, though, as at Holy Trinity, Hull, and at St Botolph's, Boston, they may never have been monasteries. They might have housed a number of chantry priests as well as the vicar, and Ottery St Mary, in Devon, is a good example. One of the finest, Edington, in Wiltshire, had a priory attached to it. The stateliest Decorated parish church, within and without, that I know is at Patrington in Yorkshire. It sails in honey-coloured

The central tower of Wells had begun to slip almost as soon as it was completed in 1322, and these vast double 'strainer' arches were urgently brought in to prop it up. They combine the most extreme stripping down of Gothic structure – no capitals, continuous mouldings, positively brutal portholes in the spandrels – with the most thrilling fluency of Gothic space, pulling all parts of the church visually together in spite of the thickness of the piers.

The twisting forest-foliage space of Wells was transformed into the unified hall church of the Perpendicular grid at the abbey of Gloucester, where a wholesale rebuilding programme was financed by the flood of pilgrims come to worship the murdered King Edward II. The King's tomb however is still in the purest Decorated of c.1330, with an effigy in alabaster on a Purbeck marble chest, under an elaborate cascade of ogee-headed niches, with the special refinement of cusps within cusps.

limestone like a ship over the flat estuary land at the mouth of the Humber. Inside it is even more magnificent than its outside would lead you to believe, a many-vistaed building of carved stone.

These building operations of the Decorated period were confined mainly to where building stone was either available or could be floated down rivers. This means that the finest churches were along the limestone belt which stretches diagonally across England from North East to South West. Every tower of the Decorated period had a spire on top of it to steady the weight of the bells when they rocked inside the tower in the bell chamber. It also steadied the external pressure of the walls of the tower. The earliest spires rose straight from the square walls of the tower and came to a point, and the edges of these spires were bevelled. They were called broach spires.

Later the base of the spire was concealed by a parapet round the tower walls. Northamptonshire and Rutland and Leicester are counties which are particularly rich in stone spires. One village built one and the neighbouring village was not to be beaten in the race to have the best spire. They became landmarks for huntsmen. The word steeplechase comes from the spires of the Midland counties.

But in the parts where there was little building stone, places like Sussex, Wiltshire and East Anglia, only flint and timber were available and towers were capped with wooden spires and a lot of the humble Norman architecture remained. These parts of the country were biding their time.

The Decorated style came to its maturity in Exeter Cathedral, which began in 1275, stylistically as well as chronologically, where Lincoln left off, and initiated a century of brilliant development in the West Country. By comparison with the sparse geometry of Early English, Exeter is prolific and luxuriant, the leitmotif *being the palm-branch effect of the continuous tierceron vaults, an abundance of vaulting ribs pouring forth from an equal abundance of clustered shafts on each column.*

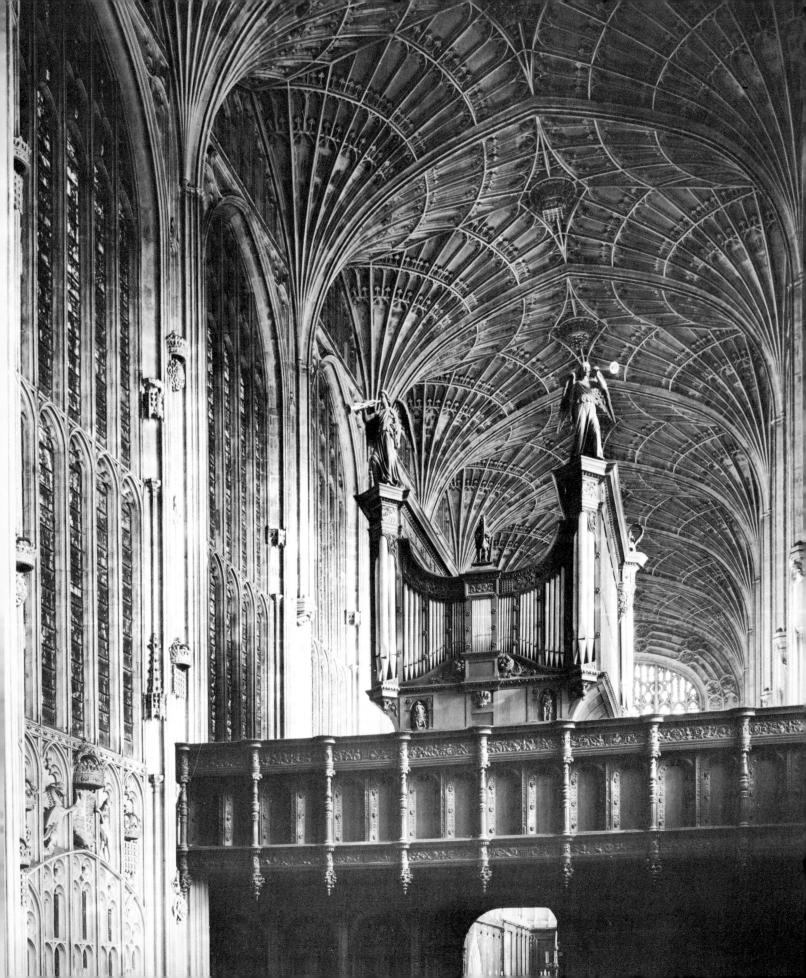

Perpendicular

PERPENDICULAR ARCHITECTURE lasted longer than any other of the English Gothic styles. It went on from the reign of Richard II to the death of Henry VIII in 1547. That is being far too precise about it because, of course, in many cottages and churches in England the style went on right until the 18th century. And, indeed, it might be possible to say that farm buildings, barns and big granaries were built in the Perpendicular manner as late as the 19th century.

People used to think it started with a burst in the Severn Valley, when the south transept of Gloucester Cathedral was remodelled in 1331 in what was then the new style. This was over 40 years before Richard II came to the throne and everyone was building in the Perpendicular manner.

Recent researchers have found that the style originated in France and was first tried out in England in the royal palace of Westminster, and in the chapter house of old St Paul's. It began as a court style. Hundreds of English churches were built in the Perpendicular manner. There are few medieval buildings in England without some traces of the style.

Perpendicular is a good name for it, for the style consists of tall vertical lines in the way of columns supporting arches and tracery in windows and stone panelling on walls.

The Victorians used to think that Early English was pure and earnest, that Decorated was the full flowering of perfection, and that Perpendicular came when architecture was beginning to go out. They often thought that things in the middle were better than things on either side.

The truth is, however, that the Perpendicular period gave us most of the best architecture we have of any period – for instance the choir and lady chapel of Gloucester Cathedral (1330 to 1457); King's College Chapel, Cambridge (1446 to 1515); St George's Chapel, Windsor (about 1480 to 1537); St Mary's Redcliffe, Bristol; St Mary's, Beverley, Yorkshire; and the supreme naves of Winchester Cathedral (1396 to 1450) and Canterbury (1379 to 1405).

It gave us the great flint churches of Norfolk and Suffolk with their carved benches, painted screens, and timber roofs adorned with angels. It gave us the towers of Somerset, the woodwork of Devon and Cornwall, and finally Bell Harry Tower (1493 to 1497) in Canterbury Cathedral, along with Bath Abbey (1501 to 1539) and the wool churches of the Cotswolds, like Cirencester, Chipping Campden and Northleach. Its crowning achievement for most people is Henry VII's chapel to Westminster Abbey.

The Perpendicular became more of a secular style than the earlier forms of Gothic. It went with rich laymen, trade guilds, merchants, weavers and sheep farmers. It did not go with monasteries and monks, though of course they used the style; but this was a time when parish churches were beginning to rival abbeys and even secular cathedrals in splendour. The friars, who were orders of preaching and itinerant priests founded in the 14th century to counteract heresy and to preach hellfire and put new life into religion, required large naves in which to preach.

Religion permeated the life of medieval

England. There was deep devotion in the late Middle Ages to Mary the Mother of God. If a church was not dedicated to her then it usually had to have a lady chapel added to it. Although villages and towns were growing in size, the largest building except for the castle was still the church. It was the chief building of every parish, the house of God. It was also the centre of the life of the community, fulfilling the role of town hall, theatre and school, as well as place of worship.

ABOVE *The business-like consistency of Perpendicular was particularly well suited to cloisters. Prior Chillenden's at Canterbury Cathedral, begun c.1395, has one of the finest lierne vaults. Its star patterns are anchored by no less than 825 heraldic bosses, a roll-call of every leading family in Kent.*

LEFT *Placed decisively across the centre of York Minster, as in most English cathedrals, is the massive stone screen called the pulpitum, with only a narrow doorway leading through into the choir. The York pulpitum, completed c.1500, consists of a stylized portrait gallery of English kings, set under elaborate niches, with the dramatic ogee arch of the dark central doorway providing a scenic atmosphere unusual in Late Perpendicular.*

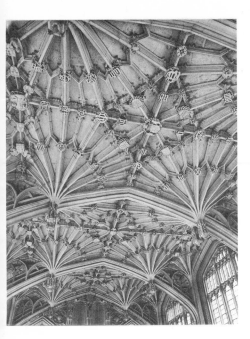

ABOVE *At the Divinity Schools at Oxford University the delicious net of lierne vaulting with pendants gives the illusion of being held in space by some kind of modern tensile structure. It was erected in 1480 by William Orchard.*

OPPOSITE *At the Cistercian abbey of Forde in Dorset, the last incumbent, Thomas Chard, elected in 1521, added to the west of the cloisters what was in effect a major country house, with a spacious great hall, extensive living chambers and a gorgeous gatehouse.*

RIGHT *The conspicuous expenditure of the new late-medieval merchant class found its expression especially in church steeples. The small Lincolnshire market town of Louth is dominated by the soaring lines of the 295-ft spire. Graceful buttresses and tall ogee-headed bell openings, with slender crocketed gables, lead the eye to the gymnastic poise of the flying buttresses supporting the spire itself, which is itself made sharp and spiky with crockets.*

The rich men of the parish built on chapels for their families and hired chantry priests to say mass for the souls of the departed of their family. In a town the guilds added chapels to the nave and kept altars in them and lights burning and hired priests to pray for the members, living and departed, of the guild. Money coming in from wool was making England very rich. In the wool districts villages vied with one another in the splendour of their churches, even more than they had done in the previous centuries. Porches were used for schools, churchyards for recreation. Gravestones were nearly all a later innovation. The poor were buried in wool, not very deep in the ground.

On feast days in the churchyard the churchwardens ordered ales, which is why to this day old inns in villages are very often near the church. There were many more holidays than there are now, sometimes several a week, and feast days went with them. In the church and outside it sacred plays were performed, and they were the beginning of the English theatre. The naves also had to be large for processions to the altars built off them. Benches were introduced for people to listen to sermons.

Light poured in from 'clear storey' windows above the nave and these windows lit the carved timbers of the

ABOVE LEFT *The mass-produced competence of Perpendicular Gothic is a reflection of the commercial origin of so many of its greatest buildings in the growth of the wool trade. It is in effect the first big-business style. The nave of Lavenham church in Suffolk, with its taut net of panelling tying arcades to clerestory and clerestory to cambered roof, is the product of such profits.*

OPPOSITE *The 15th century was one of the high points in the English art of pattern design. The 13th-century timber vault over the choir of St Alban's Cathedral was given this attractive decoration during the abbacy of John of Wheathampstead (1420–40) – hence the egotistical repetition of the eagle and the lamb, the symbols of St John the Evangelist and St John the Baptist.*

ABOVE RIGHT *The Suffolk 'wool town' of Lavenham has a more coherent sequence of opulent timber-framed houses than anywhere else in England. The group at the junction of Lady Street and Water Street includes (left) a well-preserved hall house, the Old Wool Hall, which has an open timber roof, and (right) Tudor shops with a well-preserved shop window on the corner.*

ingenious new roof, whose weight was carried down to buttresses against the exterior walls. And between the buttresses there were bigger windows. Stained glass was lighter and leading was not so thick. Yellow stain made of melted silver was a new discovery, and the prevailing colours of the new glass were white,

yellow, red, green and deep blue.

The carpenter was as important as the mason had been. The glory of the inside of the parish church, particularly in the West Country and East Anglia, was the wooden screen which shut off the priest's part from the nave. These carved wooden screens were an anglicized version of the iconostasis of the Orthodox Church. But they were not so solid as the iconostasis. Through the columns supporting the rood loft, and above the panels from which the columns sprang, you could see the vested altars and the parclose screens dividing off the separate chapels.

The screens were generally painted with saints along their bases, and then the columns were gilded and wooden columns supported a painted loft which had a staircase leading to it, from which on certain feast days, it is said, the Gospel was sung. And above the middle of the loft, in front of the high altar, there stood or hung a rood, which is a Crucifixion with the Mother of God and St John flanking it. You passed out of the nave under the figure of the crucified Lord into the chancel, where the risen Lord was in the sacrament on the altar.

The increased light showed up the intricacies of wood carving, and the crisp

lines of the thin stone columns in the nave, and the mouldings of arches and window tracery. Wall painting was less important now as there was often more glass than wall. Indeed, complete churches of the 15th century were rather like conservatories, and, had steel or cast iron been discovered in those days, the churches would probably have been executed in these materials. As it was, they made stone serve almost the same purpose as iron, so ingenious were the masons at the end of the Middle Ages in the art of thrust and counter-thrust. The Perpendicular style is engineering in stone and glass.

Of course, not all parishes could afford to have Perpendicular glass-houses, like such magnificent examples as Fairford in Gloucestershire and St Neot in Cornwall, each with its medieval windows, Southwold in Suffolk, Thaxted in Essex, or Cawston in Norfolk. But nearly every parish could afford at least one big window in the new style, and space somewhere for a family or guild altar.

This was how the parish showed that the church was not any longer under the monasteries. It had become the church of the people. Let us follow them out of the church into the streets and villages.

Elizabethan

THE VICTORIANS thought Elizabethan architecture 'debased'. But at the beginning of this century Elizabethan became very popular. It was the homely style. Later it was associated with copper warming pans, horse brasses, and electric log fires, and the novels of Dornford Yates, Jeffrey Farnol and Warwick Deeping.

It may well be that in reaction to the clinical glass boxes of the 1950s it may even come in for a revival. All the same, the great Elizabethan houses, like Longleat (1567 to 1579) and Burghley (1587), Wollaton (1588) and, most of all, Hardwick Hall (1597) – 'Hardwick Hall, more glass than wall' – had little in common with what Osbert Lancaster has well described as 'Roadhouse Tudor': they are more like the glass boxes, externally at any rate, than people realize.

From the reign of Henry VIII to that of Charles I very few churches were built, but a great many houses. The house builders of that time were no longer monarchs and ecclesiastics and barons,

but statesmen, courtiers, diplomats and merchants. Families like Cecil, Cavendish, Thynne, Tresham and Gresham come to the fore. Queen Elizabeth, always careful over cash, preferred to let her subjects build great houses for her and her court to stay in.

What the monarch and the new aristocrats started, the rest of the country followed. The richest man of every parish would try to build himself a manor house, with his coat of arms in stone over the entrance porch, and tall windows with vertical stone mullions and horizontal transoms, and the glass in leaded panes. And very charming these old houses are, with their battlemented roofs in the

earlier examples, and gabled roofs in the later ones, and their hint of the Renaissance style of the Low Countries in cornices and in classical columns of stone on either side of the entrance door and of wood over the chimneypiece.

Their builders commemorated themselves after death in stone rather than with chantry priests saying mass for their souls. Painted monuments were erected in parish churches in what were once chantry chapels. Ruffed Elizabethans were on their knees, or lay in court dress on their elbows, or on their backs, while a marble temple towered above them.

The skill of the builders of such marvels as Henry VII's chapel in West-

OPPOSITE *Though partly of Henry VII's reign, Little Moreton Hall is mostly of 1559, with a noisy gaggle of polygonal bays towards the courtyard and an even madder entrance front, facing the visitor across the moat with overhangs in all directions, arbitrary patterns like a giant's game of noughts-and-crosses, and the most extraordinary warping of the timbers.*

RIGHT *Almost certainly designed by Robert Smythson, Hardwick Hall is the climax of his development towards a synthesis of basically Gothic ideas of fenestration with basically Renaissance ideas of symmetrical layout. The central hall is now at right-angles to the entrance front and entered symmetrically at one end.*

minster Abbey went by descent into the building of houses. We begin to know more than just the names of architects but something about their personalities and families. Mark Girouard in his renowned book on Robert Smythson, the architect of Longleat, Hardwick and other great houses, quotes a passage from Sir Philip Sidney's *Arcadia* (1590) which described an Elizabethan's idea of the restrained and perfect house:

'. . . built of fair and strong stone, not affecting so much any extraordinary kind of fineness as an honourable representing of a firm stateliness; the lights, doors, and stairs rather directed to the use of the guest than to the eye of the artificer, and yet as the one chiefly heeded, so the other not neglected; each place handsome without curiosity, and homely without loathsomeness; not so dainty as not to be trod on, nor yet slubbered up with good fellowship; all more lasting than beautiful, but that the consideration of the exceeding lastingness made the eye believe it was exceeding beautiful.'

The carpenter who had constructed timber roofs of Perpendicular churches, the wood-carver of rood screens, and the stone-carver of capitals and mouldings, turned their skills to adorning the house, and the chief room in it – the dining hall, with its wooden screen and panelling, its long oak tables, its raftered roof and Renaissance stone chimneypiece.

The first phase of 16th- and early 17th-century architecture is more properly called Tudor, and starts with collegiate building and schools, and places like the Tudor part of Cardinal Wolsey's Hampton Court Palace. The plan was usually a quadrangle with an entrance tower which was a memory of the fortified castles of the Middle Ages. Prominent in the courtyard on the right or left were the dining hall and chapel. Compton Wynyates, Knole, Kirby Hall, Burghley and Longleat are on this quadrangular plan. The smaller houses often became a façade only. That is to say, the front looked like the entrance to a college or large house, with a central projecting porch and room above, and projecting wings, and a hall to right or left as you went in. But there was no quadrangle behind, and the chapel was the family chapel in the adjacent parish church, approached through a door in the garden wall.

They were built of limestone, in all its variety of colour, from Yorkshire across the Midlands to Somerset and Dorset; of brick and timber or plaster and timber, or of flint with stone dressings, in East Anglia, Kent and Worcestershire; of granite in Cornwall; of red sandstone and dark local stones in the North West. And these 17th-century manor houses are still the part of the country landscape which is most loved. Their hospitable interiors are hinted at in a delightful anonymous 17th-century poem from Christ Church, Oxford, called *The Guest*, which begins:

Yet if his majesty, our Sovereign lord,
Should of his owne accord
Friendly himselfe invite,
And say I'll be your guest tomorrowe night,

LEFT *Rebuilt after a fire in 1567 in an elaborately fantastical Tudor style which still shows in the skyline, Longleat in Wiltshire was in 1572–80 given a completely new wrap-round façade. It set a new style for the Elizabethans in its compact four-square plan, with internal courtyards only as light wells, and its outward-looking display of rippling bay windows.*

OPPOSITE ABOVE *Though still approached romantically over a moat, the entrance to Hampton Court Palace is in every other way typical of Tudor enlightenment, crisply symmetrical and generously fenestrated as well as using the sensible local material of brick. This main front achieves a masterly compromise between Renaissance symmetry and Gothic detail, with the brickwork patterned in criss-cross diapers of blue against red, under a skyline of exuberantly twisted chimneystacks.*

OPPOSITE BELOW *'Knole is neither sublime nor picturesque,' says John Newman. 'It is, however, especially in the distant view, authentic, looking almost exactly now as it did in the year Thomas Sackville died.' (1608). In fact the core of the great three-courtyard mansion is much older, built by Archbishop Thomas Bourchier in 1456–64. Thomas Sackville, 1st Earl of Dorset, improved it all round – for example, the symmetrical composition of shaped gables and towers on the south front – as well as inserting a gorgeous suite of staterooms.*

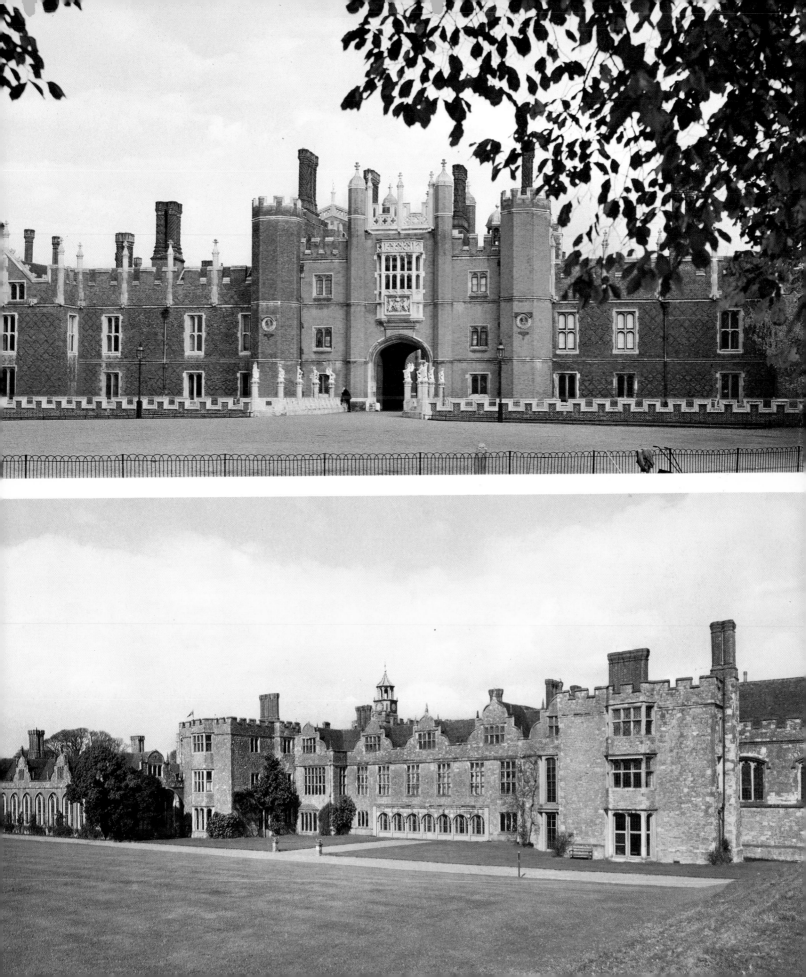

How should we stir ourselves, call and
   command
All hands to worke! 'Let no man idle stand.
Set me fine Spanish tables in the hall,
See they be fitted all;
Let there be roome to eate,
And order taken that there want no meate.
See every sconce and candlestick made
   bright,
That without tapers they may give a light,
Looke to the presence: are the carpets
   spred,
The dazie o'er the head,
The cushions in the chayre,
And all the candles lighted on the stairs?
Perfume the chambers, and in any case
Let each man give attendance in his place.'

What the lord of the manor started the
farmer and the cottagers followed. The

ABOVE *At second-floor level in Hardwick Hall is
the High Great Presence Chamber. The vast airy
bay windows, the profuse plaster friezes of forest
scenes by Abraham Smith, the fruity furniture,
the monstrous mottled fireplaces – this certainly
is not culture in the Italian or even French sense
of the Renaissance, but equally certainly it has
'character'.*

BELOW *As at Longleat, Burghley House har-
nesses classical motifs to a traditional medieval
courtyard layout, but Burghley from the start*

*(c.1556–64) had an unashamedly sensational
skyline. The courtyard entrance to the traditional
screens passage of the hall is reared up like a cobra
into a monstrous frontispiece (added 1585), with
a silhouette of obelisks and lions.*

RIGHT *The superb barrel-vaulted ceiling of the
long gallery at Chastleton House, Oxfordshire,
shows how the Elizabethans combined the Perpendicular Gothic tradition of all-over panelling
grids with the new Flemish import of strapwork
patterns.*

17th century was the time of the village
street, when the wooden hovels of the
Middle Ages were rebuilt in more durable
material, as the cloth trade prospered and
England grew richer. Many people who
have an old cottage which they think goes
back 800 years are probably living in one
which was rebuilt in the 17th century.
The old walled cities were beginning to
burst their gates.

If one can divide what is called
generically 'Elizabethan' into periods,
one might say that the Tudor period
lasted from 1485 through the reign of
Henry VIII and during the troubled
times of Edward VI and Bloody Mary,
when little building was done. The
Elizabethan period was from 1558 to
1603; from then until about 1620 the

period was Jacobean. It had its phases full of exuberance in the time of Shakespeare.

With the terrors of Philip II of Spain and his Armadas out of the way, and trade prospering with the Netherlands, England built in a style of its own which was nothing like the severe classicism that was then building in Italy. In fact, nobody wanted to be like the feared Papal countries. Instead they went in for fantasy as is seen on the roofs of Burghley, where chimneys disguised as Doric columns abound, or the roof of Longleat, with its fanciful stacks and domes in stone.

The rising excitement of the time, while restraining itself in the almost churchlike exterior walls, could not help bursting out on the roof. There was much exuberance inside the house. There is little to touch the elaboration of the hall screen at Audley End, 1615, or the long picture gallery with its Old Testament scenes in plaster at Lanhydrock in Cornwall, and the beautifully restored long gallery of Burton Agnes in Yorkshire with its tremendous wooden staircase.

This was a joyful, confident period. The equivalent of it in our history is the Victorian period at the time of the 1851 Exhibition and after, when England felt again on top of the world. It had, at moments, a similar vulgarity. Towards the end of the Elizabethan period the rough Renaissance detail from the Netherlands, which the rich were using on their gables and doors and fireplaces, and even all over the outside, as at Kirby Hall and Wollaton, was going out of fashion. Restraint and a return to the plain Perpendicular of late medieval England was coming in. You may see it in the many-windowed simplicity of Wootton Lodge, Staffordshire (1608), and in the merchants' houses of Elizabethan and Jacobean cloth towns, like Lavenham, Chipping Campden and Burford.

It was a short step from this to the restraint and proportion of those pioneers of the revival of the architecture of ancient Rome, such as Alberti (1404–1472) and Palladio (1518–1580).

LEFT *Oundle, in Northamptonshire, has two impressive inns in the Elizabethan–Jacobean tradition; but whereas the Talbot is dated 1625, the White Lion is as late as 1661, thus admirably illustrating the provincial time-lag.*

ABOVE *The black-and-white timberwork of the Midlands was as indiscriminate a mode of ostentatious self-advertisement for the Elizabethans as it was for the Victorians; the*

Elizabethans' article has merely had longer to mellow. Robert Dudley, Earl of Leicester, the Queen's favourite, took over in 1571 the late-15th-century premises in Warwick of the guilds of Holy Trinity and St George, and vamped them up to make Leycester's Hospital. The long varied frontage composes deliciously on the steeply sloping road with the medieval Westgate and its chapel (and the chapel's Victorian staircase).

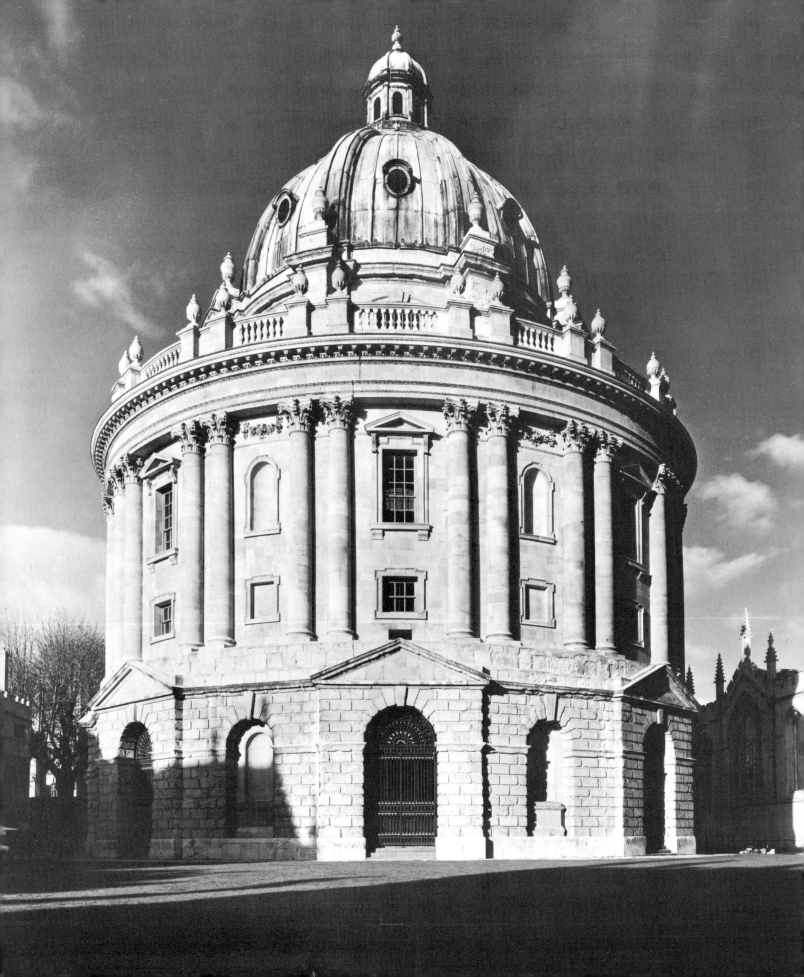

Renaissance

THE WHOLE SCHEME of medieval education may be seen displayed in stone and paint in Oxford. In the old Bodleian quadrangle were the old schools. Painted names of the subjects taught in them are over the doors. By one route undergraduates entered for lectures on various branches of Medicine. By the other route they learned Jurisprudence and what came to be known as the polite arts. But both schools of learning led to final graduation in Theology. This was in the Divinity School, which occupied one side of the quadrangle.

It is one of the most delicate late Gothic buildings in England. Facing it, as you come out, and closing the fourth side of the quadrangle, is the Tower of the Five Orders, which was built later in the reign of James I. It symbolizes the New Learning, the return to ancient Rome from Christendom. The Five Orders are Doric, Ionic and Corinthian, which were used by the Greeks, and Tuscan, a Roman version of Doric, and Composite, a Roman mixture of Ionic and Corinthian.

The sturdy Doric is plain and has an unobtrusive capital. The slender Ionic has a capital topped with ram's horns (called volutes) and the rich Corinthian has a big capital which looks like fern leaves topped with bracken shoots carved in stone.

A knowledge of the Five Orders was essential to a man of taste in England from about 1650 until 1950. In Italy the Five Orders had been studied for two centuries; even the word 'taste' was unknown until the Renaissance.

The strict rules about the proportion of columns to their capitals and bases, their

ABOVE *The tower at the entrance to the Bodleian Library, Oxford (built 1613–18), is still in reality a late-medieval gatehouse, which has then fixed to it the Greek and Roman Doric, Tuscan, Ionic, Composite and Corinthian Orders in an ascending crescendo of scholarship.*

OPPOSITE *The Radcliffe Library at Oxford, the so-called Radcliffe Camera, shows James Gibbs at his most Baroque, recalling in the details of its dome not so much Wren's St Paul's as St Peter's at Rome. The actual library is a domed room at first-floor level in the drum, over a ground floor which originally was a paved piazza for conversation, with its entrance arches open to the air.*

diameters, the entablatures above them, the mouldings throughout the building, proportions of window to wallspace, height to base, and height of first storey, and height of attic, were all worked out, with variants, according to set rules.

The first rules originated from a treatise by a 1st-century Roman architect called Vitruvius, which was discovered in a monastic library in the 16th century. That discovery, and what derived from it, has influenced all European and North American architecture and much Imperial architecture to the present day. It was not until the 1920s that an intimate knowledge of the Five Orders was given up as an essential part of an architect's training. The rules were not arbitrary but they could only be varied by a genius. In England they were varied by such men as Wren, Hawksmoor, Vanbrugh and provincial architects who through well-intentioned ignorance stumbled on a style of their own.

The word 'provincial' as a term meaning slightly inferior must be a Renaissance conception, dating from the time when it was the fashion to think ancient Rome was the fount of all aesthetic knowledge. It is in the 17th century too that the word 'Gothic', meaning the work of ignorant vandals, who were the Goths, was applied to the medieval architecture of the pointed arch.

I once asked Sir John Summerson, the coolest, most lucid and accomplished of all living writers on English architecture, about the difference between Renaissance architecture and Gothic. Was it, I said, 'that the medieval builders thought in terms of the plan first, and left the exterior to be determined by the plan, and did the Renaissance people design the façades first and fit the rooms in afterwards?' He said no: the difference was that Gothic architects were masons, who thought in terms of stone and construction, and Renaissance architects were sketchers who thought in terms of ink on parchment or paper.

The truth of this is certainly borne out by Inigo Jones, born in Smithfield, London, of humble parentage, who is

thought the first to have introduced to this country a whole building in the Renaissance style. He was a designer of masques in the Court of King James I, and went to Italy, where he saw the new Roman or Renaissance-style buildings on the spot.

First he introduced the style into the scenery for his masques, and of course all courtiers – that is to say men of taste from the monarch downwards – knew the style; he then interpreted it in stone, and

RIGHT *When George Vernon began in 1665 to remodel the Jacobean Sudbury Hall, Derbyshire, he was not quite yet in the latest fashion of Dutch brick classicism. He altered the window tracery to a strange bastardized pattern neither Jacobean nor classical, but then remodelled the staircase (1675–6) with the most up-to-date London craftsmen: Edward Pierce for the wood carving, Bradbury and Pettifer for the plasterwork. The Baroque ceiling paintings by Louis Laguerre were added in 1691.*

BELOW *Wren's remodelling of the eastern end of Hampton Court Palace in 1689–1702 for William*

and Mary is, in its limitations as well as in its merits, a perfect expression of the bloodless revolution which had made the monarchy democratic. It is beautifully detailed in its parts (the noble stateroom windows on the first floor, the circular and square-windowed attics above), it is

cheerily domestic in its red brick warmth and Portland stone trim, and it is emphatically not grand in the Versailles way.

OPPOSITE *The most exacting intellectually of Wren's fifty improvisations on the theme of a parish church, St Stephen's, Walbrook, shows the coolly scientific Englishman clothing the utmost inventiveness in an almost offhand classical vocabulary. Everything is subordinated to the subtle unification of three totally different kinds of church: the longitudinal basilica with aisles, the Greek cross with equal transepts and the circular domed rotunda.*

it is generally thought that the Queen's House at Greenwich, which he designed in his capacity of Surveyor to the Royal Works, was the first complete Renaissance building to be seen in the country.

When you come to think that all the rest of the cities in England were composed of narrow lanes with gabled roofs and no regularity, such as still may be seen in the streets near cathedrals of cities like Canterbury, Durham, Norwich and Lincoln, you will realize how strange, even outrageous, was a three-dimensional building in white Portland stone, with a plainness about it that had not been seen in England since the days of castles and fortified dwellings. Art historians are inclined to think that the first is the best. If this were always true, then the Renaissance work in England by Inigo Jones, such as the piazza in Covent Garden and the additions to Wilton in Wiltshire, would be the best English Renaissance of all.

In truth, a more delightful architect of the new style was Sir Christopher Wren, a clever young Oxford mathematician and scientist, son of a High Church Dean of Ely, who took up architecture when he was over twenty. His bust shows a cheerful smile on his face; his character was one of integrity and patience. He was made Surveyor of the King's Works. After the Great Fire of London, in 1666, he was put in charge of the rebuilding of the City, including its many churches and patched-up Cathedral of St Paul.

First he tried redesigning in the grand Italian manner, with straight avenues leading the eye to a monolithic one-storey cathedral in the middle. (He never travelled farther abroad than France.) But he realized that the citizens of London did not want this plan of piazzas and straight lines. They wanted the narrow alleys with little courtyards and shelter from the weather and glimpses of churches that the pre-fire City had provided.

Wren built his new cathedral in two storeys, limiting the height of the houses in the City to below that of the first storey of his cathedral. After he had rebuilt the

ABOVE *Wren's vast enterprises in the City of London, particularly St Paul's, succeeded in permeating the provincial building industry with their first new tradition for a century. Christopher Kempster, a Wren mason, built the exceedingly handsome town hall at Abingdon, Berkshire, which he could well have designed too. The plan is simple – an open market arcade with a single court room above – while the vocabulary is that of the most fashionable country houses.*

OPPOSITE *The Queen's House at Greenwich has a misleadingly cool composure, fulfilling too easily the expectation of a perfect model of Palladian discipline. But in 1617, a year after its design, a letter refers to 'some curious devise' of Inigo Jones – this being the fact that the house actually consisted of two separate blocks connected by a bridge over what was then the main Dover road. It ran where the Regency colonnade runs now. John Webb, Jones' son-in-law, put two more bridges across in 1662, thus giving the house the solid cubic form it now has from a distance.*

ABOVE *The 17th-century idea of the garden was still of a highly artificial pleasaunce (Dutch, Italian or French) extending the civilized domesticity of the house a short distance from it but no further. The fabulous topiary at the Elizabethan mansion of Levens Hall, Westmorland, is late in date (c.1700) but exceptionally complete – and the work of a Frenchman.*

LEFT *Internally the Queen's House, Greenwich, as completed in 1635, shows Jones' Palladianism at its purest: geometrically proportioned rooms, sparsely decorated with ovolo friezes, garlands and gilt door frames. The climax is the acrobatically flying Tulip Staircase, so called from the scroll pattern in the wrought-iron balustrade.*

bodies of the City churches round St Paul's he added towers and steeples, some in lead and some in Portland stone, to lead the eye as it lifted out of the alleys to the skyline and to the dome of his new Cathedral.

Until the middle of the last century, when the restrictions on heights of buildings were relaxed so that landlords might make more money, the skyline of the City of London seen above the Thames must have been the most beautiful in Europe. We can see this from the paintings of Canaletto and hear it from Wordsworth's sonnet 'Composed upon Westminster Bridge'.

Wren's greatest achievement was his work in the City. There he adapted the Renaissance style to the English climate; instead of slavishly copying the Italian, he designed steeples and towers to churches which were reminiscent of the Gothic steeples that had been on them before the

fire. The most notable is that of St Mary-le-Bow, Cheapside. Sometimes he went so far as to design in Gothic. Tom Tower is his addition to the skyline of Oxford.

His assistant Nicholas Hawksmoor was an equally talented man, but in a more grand and sumptuous way than that of the cheerful Wren. He designed the mausoleum at Castle Howard, and the mighty churches of the East End of London – St George's in the East, Christ Church, Spitalfields and St Ann, Limehouse – which sail like battleships in Portland stone over the brick chimney pots of the East End.

Equally tremendous, and rather more theatrical, was the work of Sir John Vanbrugh, the playwright who took up architecture. He designed Blenheim and the house of Castle Howard, and worked at Greenwich, whose hospital is the finest assembly of the architecture of this period that we possess.

Men like Wren, Vanbrugh and Hawksmoor were patronized by monarchs and noblemen, who could afford to build the new style in Portland stone. Lesser architects, and sometimes these architects themselves, used brick, which since Tudor times had been the cheapest unit of building in clay districts like London and East Anglia, and parts of Yorkshire and Worcestershire. The gap between an architect, in the sense of a man who sketched out a design, and a builder, was then very wide. Architecture was not a profession, it was a polite accomplishment. The builder interpreted as best he could the designs which had been sketched out by his employer.

For this reason many excellent Classical country houses, town halls and brick mansions and streets, which are attributed to Wren and his like, are often the work of clever masons who took up the new style and used it very often with as much skill as their masters.

If Wren had designed as many buildings as are ascribed to him, he would have been as ubiquitous as Queen Elizabeth I and all the beds she is supposed to have slept in.

OPPOSITE *In spite of a fire in 1940, the great hall of Castle Howard is still one of the most thrilling spaces in England, and without doubt the most Baroque in its vertiginous twists of space and exaggerations of scale. It is a simple Greek cross in plan, punctuated by huge fluted piers; to the left of the entrance the arm of the cross is occupied by a gigantic fireplace, to the right by an equally gigantic recess for a statue. On each side a grand staircase rises behind fireplace or recess as though taking off through a forest, the visitor gradually emerging from behind the sculptured skyline onto broad stretches of balcony at the upper level, enclosed by superb iron railings.*

ABOVE *Sir John Vanbrugh's architectural career seems to have started with implausible suddenness,*

with his startling commissions for Castle Howard and Blenheim Palace. His assistant Nicholas Hawksmoor (recruited from Wren's office) said of Blenheim that on the practical side 'all of them could not Stir an Inch without me', yet he, Hawksmoor, was 'like a loving Nurse that almost thinks the Child her own' – that is to say, Vanbrugh was the real begetter.

BELOW *The Dutch box of Charles II's reign in the end became the modest vernacular-Baroque brick house of the country town. Clarence House at Thaxted, Essex, which stands opposite the church, has lead rainwater heads dated 1715. Typical of the Baroque influence is the slight upturn of the frieze under the entrance doorway pediment.*

Georgian

ONE PATRON OF MEN like Inigo Jones and Wren was the monarchy. The Stuarts encouraged the Palladian style, named after Andrea Palladio (1518–80), who wrote an illustrated treatise on how to build in the Classical or Roman fashion. Though the Stuarts introduced the Classical style to England, their richer subjects were the chief patrons of it. (Except for Windsor and Buckingham Palace, royal residences are comparatively modest. And Buckingham Palace externally is no Versailles.)

The great houses of the nobility, most of whom were large landowners, exceeded in splendour the royal residences. Queen Victoria talked about going from 'my house' to 'your palace' when she called on the Duke of Sutherland at what is now called Lancaster House from her own palace of St James's. Tremendous buildings, mostly in an English version of Baroque, such as Vanbrugh's Blenheim (1705–20), and his Castle Howard (1699–1726), Flitcroft's Wentworth Woodhouse (1735–70) and Stowe are exceptions from

what most of us mean by the English Georgian country house. This is thought of as something plain, cube-shaped and set in a park, diversified with woods, pasture and a stretch of water.

The shape and plan of these houses derives from the Queen's House at Greenwich, which itself derives from Palladio's rules about how to build in the Classical style. The base must look solid, the first floor has the larger windows. The plan is clearly described by John Harris in his excellent booklet on Georgian country houses – 'an oblong divided in two on the long or horizontal axis, and in three on the short or vertical axis, resulting in six rooms with a communicating hall and saloon in the centre'.

There were at least two doors to every room and the rooms were so arranged that you could walk right round the house on its chief floor by going from room to

room. Doors were placed so that they would not knock furniture as you opened them. The proportion of the outside of the house was echoed in the room. There would be a skirting round the walls to suggest a solid base. The walls were thought of as a background for pictures, and one picture was the view from the window itself into the park. The ceiling was a compensation for the lack of Italian sky and was diversified with plasterwork and sometimes paintings. The focus of attention on the walls was the chimneypiece and the gilt looking glass above it.

The outside of the house was regular with a central feature of, let us say, three windows in the middle on the main front. This central feature would be emphasized either by a slight projection from the main block or by an entrance door or a portico with columns. The rear elevation on this front was much the same, only the central feature might be differently emphasized.

Any floors above the first floor were slightly smaller than those below. The whole cube was bound together at the top by a projecting cornice, and between the ground and first floor by a band of stone. The building might be topped by a balustraded or solid parapet hiding the roofs and chimneys. In early 18th-century examples of this sort of house, the eaves were at times brought right down to the cornice. Then the attic or gable windows and chimney stacks were turned into decorative features and made part of the proportion of the whole exterior.

If these country houses were to be bigger, they had to be extended symetrically. If you had a wing on one side, you added a

OPPOSITE *Syon House, an Elizabethan mansion, was transformed by Robert Adam in 1761 into a novel domestic environment. He devised an elegant and sensuous synthesis of the neoclassicist's discoveries on the Grand Tour, including the murals of Pompeii and the Etruscan tombs. His fastidious miniaturising is shown in the ceiling of the Red Drawing Room.*

RIGHT *Frederick Hervey, Earl of Bristol and Bishop of Derry, was one of the more eccentric graduates of the Grand Tour. Central rotundas were evidently an obsession with him. Ickworth (begun 1793, and eventually fitted out c.1830) was designed primarily for external show, with many strange-shaped rooms fitted into the arbitrary oval. The architect was Frederick Sandys.*

similar wing on the other. People with plenty of money to spare would even have a kitchen wing separate from the main part of the house and connected to it (to please the eye) by a colonnade. The food would be brought by underground passages from the kitchen wing to the basement of the centre block. To balance the composition on the other side of the house, a colonnade would lead to the stable block. Most Georgian houses consisted of the central block alone with stables and a walled fruit garden separated from the house by trees or the lie of the land.

In stone or brick, according to the quarries or kilns in the district, these houses rose up in every county. They either took the place of an earlier manor house near the church, or were sited between parishes on unenclosed land. Commons and forests disappeared. Tenantry were housed in farms also built on Palladian principles, and if the landlord were rich enough, sometimes whole villages were created by the squire for his tenants.

In these Palladian days of landlord and tenant, in the agricultural parts of England, the architect did not think, as he often has to do today, entirely in terms of the house he was building. He saw it as part of the landscape around it. It had to make two impressions. One was that the visitor approaching it must think that it was rather larger than it was. There would be a gate lodge and a winding drive giving occasional glimpses now of the house, now of the lake and of seemingly endless forest. The front door would, of course, be the imposing finale. The other aspect he had to consider was that of the squire who had paid for the house. The views from the windows of his chief rooms of entertainment must give the impression

The great Elizabethan mansion of Audley End in Essex has a Capability Brown landscape of 1763 studded with the delectable temples which expressed the Georgian pride of ownership. Robert Adam's Tea House of 1783 is unexpectedly situated over a bridge, an almost Chinese composition detailed in an elegant neo-classicism.

Stourhead, the greatest of the Georgian landscape gardens, consists of a continuous promenade round an irregularly-sided triangular lake, along the edge of which the banker Henry Hoare created a series of complicated landscape pictures, with Palladian temples. The Temple of Flora (Henry Flitcroft, 1745) was one of the first of these.

The Palladian mansion of Prior Park was designed by the elder John Wood in 1735, on a hill overlooking Bath, for Ralph Allen, the quarry-owner who transformed the Roman spa. Wood used pliable Bath stone to achieve his own brand of Roman Revival, with noble streets set in the midst of civilized landscape as Prior Park was.

that he owned everything in sight. This could be done by planting a wood between himself and a neighbour's territory. In order to distract the eye of a guest from an unworthy object, a Classical temple could be set on a hill, looking rather like a copy of that in the landscape after Claude Lorraine which the squire had bought on his Grand Tour of Europe.

The admiration of ancient Rome was not confined to the country districts and those rich enough to build Palladian villas in them. The word 'villa' in Palladian terms included the country round it. The taste spread to the towns. The merchant would leave his residence above his office and build his Palladian villa in the fields outside the city. The rector would rebuild his rectory and plant an irregular garden with winding paths. Even the lawyer and

the apothecary would build their Palladian villas, using the local builder who had, like the squire's architect, got his patterns of how to build correctly from the many books available with engraved plates of designs for temples, small or large villas, lodges, bridges, grottos and palaces. These were published throughout the 18th century and may still be bought in secondhand bookshops.

The style of Palladian architecture changed greatly during the 18th century as the different architects and different sorts of decoration and furniture came into fashion. Estate carpenters became skilled cabinetmakers. Thomas Chippendale of Nostell is the most famous example.

It is difficult to lay down rules for dating Palladian buildings, though you may reasonably assume that London took the lead and other places followed, so that the farther a place is from London, the safer it is to allow for a time lag of ten to twenty years. At the beginning of the century, plasterwork inside and stone mouldings and festoons outside are carved more in the round than they were later. They are

thicker, as are the wooden bars that hold the panes of glass.

After 1750 the work of Sir William Chambers and the Scotsmen Robert and James Adam changed public taste. Lord Burlington and his friend William Kent, the architect, furniture designer and landscaper, had dictated what was good taste, and at the acme are Chiswick House, Middlesex, and Mereworth Castle, Kent – domed Italian villas which would have looked as well outside Venice as London. And perhaps the chief difference between the 18th-century man of taste and his equivalent, if he exists, today, is that the architect would rough out what he wanted in the way of a house to the mason and the plasterer, to the joiner he would rough out the panelling, and to the cabinetmaker the furniture. There was a rule of thumb about mouldings and proportions and anyhow it was all in the engraved books available, so that the architect knew roughly what he would see.

By the middle of the 18th century, designers such as Chambers and the brothers Adam advocated chastity in design. Plasterwork inside the house was made much flatter, colours were subdued as in Wedgwood pottery. Mouldings both inside and outside were reduced to a minimum. There was great insistence on proportion. Glazing bars in windows were thinner than they had been; panes of glass were larger. Surfaces were smoother. The architect in search of inspiration went farther than Palladio and looked at the products of the later Roman Empire, such as were to be seen at Spalato (Split) to which Robert Adam first drew fashionable attention. Then two other architects discarded Roman examples and sought the purest source of all from the classical world – ancient Greece. They were James Stuart and Nicholas Revett. Stuart designed Greek temples in the parks of Hagley and Shugborough in 1758. In 1778, Revett designed a new church in the Greek style at Ayot St Lawrence, Hertfordshire. The two architects published in 1762 a book on the antiquities of Athens.

The Greek style became the new fashion. Eventually houses and places of worship and public institutions were built in imitation of Greek temples. By

now, the 19th century had begun and the advanced architect of the 1800s would have thought the Palladian style of a century before corrupt. Pillars and half-pillars were attached to houses just as decoration, not as supports for the superstructure. How dishonest! In Greek buildings – especially the purest of all Greek, the original native Doric – a sturdy column, plain or fluted, with an unadorned capital and no base, could be seen to support the portico.

ABOVE *Castle Hill House at Launceston, Cornwall, is typical of the unworried mixture of Baroque and Palladian forms by the local builder. In this case the warm red brick, the broken pediment and the elaborate patterns of rustication on the stone frame of the circular window are survivals of Baroque exuberance. Yet the symmetrical* hauteur *of the house is unmistakably Palladian, as is the toga'd gentleman on top.*

MIDDLE *The crucial change in attitudes to art in the 18th century was the shift, away from geometrical ideas of beauty based on ideal proportions, towards a more emotional response to the appearances of things. The numerous Gothic follies were intended to give poetic impressions of melancholy or history; this one is at Corsham Court, Wiltshire, part of an elaborate landscape laid out by Capability Brown in 1761–4.*

BELOW *Milton Abbas in Dorset, with its gently curving street of thatched white cottages fronting onto communal lawns, looks curiously similar to the most progressive of arty-crafty garden suburbs of 1910. Yet it resulted from the most extreme kind of* ancien régime *arrogance: the Earl of Dorchester in 1770 having employed Sir William Chambers to turn the medieval abbey into a luxurious country house, was bored with the prospect of the medieval market town occupying what Capability Brown was ready to turn into flowing green lawn. So the town was neatly packed up and, with Chambers and Brown advising, was laid out anew in its little valley half-a-mile south-east.*

OPPOSITE *Lansdown Crescent (1789–93) is not, architecturally, one of the climaxes of Bath, but it is without equal as spectacular townscape. Perched perilously high up on a south-facing hillside, the terraces wriggle along the contour, first convex, then concave, then convex again. The roadway, fenced off from the houses by elegant urn-topped railings, is built up over vaults, with a sheer drop on the other side down to trees and scrub.*

Greek was not the only style open to imitation: Horace Walpole, at Strawberry Hill, Twickenham, had formed a committee of taste in the 1750s for making his house Gothic and Chinese. Why copy Rome? Why not go back to the native English style? Some years before, Kent had erected sham English castles as adornments to his garden landscapes. So had other garden architects. Why not build a whole house to Gothic taste? Of course, certain rules of proportion inherited by all civilized people must be observed. You could not very well reduce Gothic to the three chief Orders, but you could at least give it Classical proportions.

In about 1805 a nabob from India had built himself a house in the Indian style in Gloucestershire. It was called Sezincote. And the Prince Regent himself had copied the style for his Pavilion at Brighton.

OPPOSITE *James Wyatt was able to handle Adam's most refined style to even greater effect than Adam himself, applying a razor-sharp control to his spatial rhythms. The entrance hall at Heveningham Hall, Suffolk, completed in 1784, has a Roman tunnel with Adam's usual tripartite screen of columns across each end. The apple-green walls set off the paterae of white stucco and the columns of brownish scagliola.*

ABOVE *The inner sanctum of the Georgian Man of Taste was naturally his library. Situated in one of the wings which were added to Stourhead in 1793 for Sir Richard Colt Hoare, archaeologist and historian, this gently barrel-roofed room retains its original furnishings of chairs, desk, large table for holding portfolios, library steps – all purpose-made by the younger Thomas Chippendale. The lunettes at each end of the ceiling have copies of Raphael's Vatican frescoes, one in stained glass by Francis Eginton, the other painted by Samuel Woodforde.*

BELOW *The Thamesside villa of Strawberry Hill was not the absolute pioneer of the Gothick Revival which the self-publicising of its owner, Horace Walpole, proclaimed it to be. What Walpole did was to convince his visitors (opening his home to the public) that Gothic was an acceptable alternative dress to Adam's neo-classicism. The delicious Gallery designed in 1763 by Thomas Pitt, Lord Camelford, retains a classical composition of niches underneath the shimmering surface of fan-vaults and mirrors.*

Regency and Early Victorian

WHAT DETERMINES THE ARCHITECTURE of a country is the people who pay for it. At the beginning of the last century the middle classes were building themselves new houses outside the towns from which they made their money. Bankers, lawyers, merchants and land agents set up as small squires. Those who could not afford to do this removed to elegant stucco crescents and squares with Hanoverian names on the outskirts of the town – Brunswick, Coburg, Royal, Sussex, Waterloo. The Napoleonic wars put a temporary stop to foreign travel, so that spas and sea-bathing places flourished. Preoccupation with architectural style became fashionable. Books containing beautiful coloured aquatint engravings of villas, gate lodges and ornamental gardens, were published by architects. The style may have been plaster deep, yet the chic rooms inside retained spacious Georgian proportions, even if the outside were Tudor, Egyptian or Oriental. The servants were still consigned to the attics for their sleeping, and to the basement for the cooking.

The prince of architects in the 1820s was George IV's favourite, John Nash. He it was who laid out that grand architectural march in the metropolis from 'the Regent's Park', with its Grecian villas and Roman terraces and crescents, down to Regent Street; and with Regent Street he divided the slums of Soho from the more aristocratic neighbourhood of Hanover Square. At either end of his street he designed a circus, and from the Piccadilly end his street sloped down to Carlton House, where the Regent had a palace (now replaced by Carlton House Terrace) overlooking St James's Park. This was

ABOVE *Nash turned the Prince Regent's fields into the Regent's Park, lakes and woods being interspersed with grand villas and such special attractions as the zoo. Round the edge he laid out terrace houses for the wealthy, grouped flatteringly to suggest a series of vast royal palaces, Cumberland Terrace for example, built in 1826, having a liveliness of composition which quite disguises its actual division into thin vertical dwellings.*

OPPOSITE *The prosperity of Bristol was based upon its trade with the Americas and the West Indies, so it is not surprising that the elegant spa of Clifton has a strongly 'plantation' atmosphere in its endless umbrella-roofed balconies. Royal York Crescent of c.1810–20 is a splendid example of spec-building on the grand scale, propped up on the cliff's edge with its roadway built out over capacious vaults. It soon acquired the fading splendour of an* ancien régime, *the abolition of slavery coinciding with the rise of Liverpool as a successful competitor for Bristol's trade.*

turned into a picturesque garden in the Capability Brown style with a winding lake. At Cumberland Market, east of Regents Park, he laid out a square of working-class houses.

Nash did for London what the Woods had done for Bath and others had done for Edinburgh. Living in towns was becoming fashionable, and a genteel house in a crescent or square was something which set you up in the eyes of your fellow townsmen. Many a town had its Nash in the late Georgian period – Foulston in Devonport, who united that once splendid Greek town to Plymouth; Dobson and Grainger at Newcastle upon Tyne; Papworth at Cheltenham; Decimus Burton at Tunbridge Wells and St Leonard's-on-Sea; and many other local builders of distinction, who could run you up a chapel, a church, an atheneum, a hall or a villa, in any style you required. Taste was less selfish in those days than it became later. Whatever their style, late Georgian buildings usually fitted in with their neighbours and were usually designed in relation to trees, and grass.

All the designers of crescents and squares and towns and villas in these days probably looked up to Sir John Soane, the grand old man of the profession, who was chiefly instrumental in founding the Royal Institute of British Architects. He would have liked every member of the Institute to have made the Grand Tour of Europe, and scholarships were founded to help talented students to make it. Architects who were members of the Institute considered themselves artists first (with a thorough knowledge of the styles achieved through examination),

and builders second. England was already being divided by the professionalism which has now turned most of us into narrower specialists. The late Georgian architect, artist though he considered himself, would still have insisted on good building by the builder. That terrible December day in 1825 when the enormous tower designed by James Wyatt for Fonthill Abbey collapsed was not easily forgotten. There had been a dishonest clerk of the works, but the disgrace attached itself to the profession, as happened after the recent collapse of the Ronan Point flats in London. The foundation of the Royal Institute might also be seen as the beginning of a great battle in Victorian architecture, the battle of the styles. Soane had invented his own style, a kind of simplified Greek and Adam, where proportion and light and shade were more important than colour and decoration. Greek was thought to be rather limited for use in this country,

OPPOSITE *The centre of the Royal Pavilion at Brighton is still the quiet bow-fronted classical villa designed for the Prince Regent in 1786–7 by Henry Holland. What Nash did in 1815–22 was to drape over it the great-grandmother of Californian film sets: a lacey see-through garment of iron-framed stucco, consisting of cloisters and balconies, balustrades and metal-sheeted domes, all in the Islamic or Moghul vocabulary, with a few Gothic touches – a style which was usually called Hindoo.*

ABOVE *The Regency style was the first to fulfil the demands of commerce in the modern sense, and the covered shopping arcade was one of the most successful inventions of the age, albeit imported from Paris. The Royal Opera Arcade in Pall Mall was the earliest in London (1816–18), designed by John Nash, with the assistance of G. S. Repton, as part of his vast Regent Street speculation.*

BELOW *Begun in 1812, the entire scheme of Regent's Park was complete soon after 1830. Sussex Place shows Nash at his most provocative: vast scale (650 ft long, with phalanxes of Corinthian columns), exciting and rather vulgar 'features' (the whizzing curves of the inner corners, and the weird octagonal domes) and of course jerry building behind.*

though its popularity continued in Scotland until the middle of the century. Indian and Turkish and Egyptian were perhaps a bit flashy and more suitable for places of entertainment than for domestic use. But the ancient style of England, the Gothic – there was something we could all emulate, and do bigger and better than it had been done in the Middle Ages. The novels of Sir Walter Scott, far more than the Gothick novels of Mrs Radcliffe before them and the fancy Gothick of Horace Walpole's Strawberry Hill, made the Middle Ages live for early Victorian readers. So did Thomas Barham's *Ingoldsby Legends*.

There was one man in whom this early part of the battle of the styles met and resolved itself into a great and famous building. This was Sir Charles Barry (1795–1860), who designed the Houses of Parliament at Westminster. In this work he was helped over the details, particularly the woodwork, ironwork, stained glass and decoration, by A. W. N. Pugin (1812–52). Barry was the son of a prosperous Westminster stationer, who died when he was young, leaving him enough money to spend three years drawing and measuring in Greece, Italy, Egypt and Palestine. Before he went abroad he had already learned to be a surveyor, and his meticulous plans and bold attractive sketches survive in the library of the Institute. At heart Barry was a Classical man, liking the Roman style above all. He had decided opinions and said that porticos should not be stuck on to the middle of a building, as they had been by Palladian architects, but should go the whole length of a façade, and should be deep. He thought that roofs, even on Classical buildings, should be in evidence, and stone chimney stacks should be made into part of the design. He disliked the 18th-century fashion of putting statues on the roofs of palaces. This, he thought, took away from the scale of the building: statues should be on the ground. He delighted in the formal gardening of Italy, and introduced it to England at Trentham, Nottinghamshire, and Shrubland, Suffolk, whence it spread to municipal parks and squares.

When Barry returned to England in 1820 and married, he had spent all his money and had to get what work he could. At this time Tudor Gothic was coming into fashion for building new, cheap churches. Barry built some in Manchester, and St Peter's, near the Steine at Brighton, shows his concern for skyline and for a portico running along one side of a building. In 1833–6 he designed King Edward's School, Birmingham, in Tudor Gothic. In 1837 Barry designed Highclere Castle, Hampshire, in an Anglo-Italian style of his own devising. Both were foretastes of his Houses of Parliament, for whose design he won a competition after the

ABOVE *Victorian choice of architectural style usually had an evocative or symbolic logic – banks Italianate because of the Medici, cemeteries Egyptian because of the Valley of the Kings. But why should John Dobson's railway station at Monkwearmouth have been so academically Greek? Built in 1848 to celebrate the election to Parliament of George Hudson, the 'Railway King', was it an architectural gesture towards Democracy, Greek in style because of Periclean Athens?*

BELOW *Albermarle Villas at Stoke Damerel, a suburb of Plymouth, illustrate the way in which the landscape was received into the house in the form of verandas and balconies, while the house was projected into the landscape in conservatories and bow windows. The broad bracketed eaves of the villas are derived from Tuscany, or rather from the idealized farmhouses which Nash derived at second-hand from the landscape paintings of Claude.*

burning of the old Houses of Parliament in 1836.

One of the conditions of the competition was that the building should be Gothic, and that St Stephen's Hall should be retained. This enabled Barry to make a clear and brilliant plan. You enter the building through a cloister which goes past one end of Westminster Hall and opens into a stone-vaulted octagon. On one side of this is an oblong block with the House of Commons in its midst and a clock tower, housing Big Ben, on the

Clifton Suspension Bridge (1829–64) is a masterpiece of apparently effortless conquest of space, the subtly tapered pylons, the parabolic arches and the sweeping cables all, as its designer, Isambard Kingdom Brunel put it, 'made to harmonise with scenery so peculiarly suited to such a work of art'. Brunel did intend some Egyptian ornament on the pylons, and he made alternative Gothic designs, but in the end, when Hawkshaw and Barlow completed the bridge with the suspension cables salvaged from the Hungerford footbridge in London, everything followed Brunel's aim of being 'as simple and unobtrusive as possible'.

south-east corner. On the other side of the octagon a similar oblong encloses the House of Lords from which the enormous Royal Gallery leads by the Royal Stairs down to the Victoria Tower on the north-west corner of the building. The two Houses are on the same level as are all the principal rooms. Because the site is a marsh and Barry wanted to make his great palace look higher, he added prominent vertical features such as the two towers and the spires and spirelets, which give the outside of the building so varied an appearance when seen from different directions.

While he was in Birmingham Barry met Augustus Welby Pugin, much his junior, and a great enthusiast for the Gothic. He was a violent and excitable writer, a witty caricaturist of the Classical style, which he did not like (and, about which he used to argue with Barry, who used in turn to tease Pugin for the Strawberry Hill Gothick furniture that Pugin had designed for Windsor Castle, when a boy). Pugin was so enamoured of the Middle Ages that he ate off Gothic plate, made his womenfolk wear medieval dresses, and joined the Church of Rome because he thought that it would be like what English churches were like in 1440. However, most Roman Catholics in England in 1840 preferred the Classic style, and the people who paid most attention to Pugin's vigorous propaganda and attractive dreams of a holy England, full of spires, stained glass, twinkling candles and broidered copes were members of the Church of England. Pugin's contribution to the Houses of Parliament is found largely in its decoration. The plan and the outline and the style, based on Henry VII's chapel in Westminster Abbey opposite, are obviously Barry's work. Pugin died at the age of 40, mad. He completed in his short life what would have taken most people a century. His best buildings are St Chad's Roman Catholic Cathedral, Birmingham (1839–41), St Augustine's, Ramsgate (1846), and St Giles', Cheadle (1847). Barry's best buildings after the Houses of Parliament are the City Art Gallery, Manchester (1824–35, Greek), the Traveller's Club, London (1829–31), and the Reform Club next door to it (1837–41). Both clubs are subtle variants on Italian palaces.

In the National Portrait Gallery the two architects are shown on the same wall. Pugin looks ascetic and solemn, like a High Church clergyman, and not at all like the breezy, amusing man with a passion for sailing in small boats and dressing like a sailor that we know him to have been. Barry, with his prominent eyes, curly hair and smiling face, looks like a benevolent alderman and not at all the industrious, shy man he was who never left his drawing board except for the company of his wife and children. Pugin was a medievalist, a devoted Roman Catholic, and presumably an old-fashioned Tory. Barry was a Liberal and a strong Protestant. As so often happens with opposites these two men got on well together. Their families quarrelled after their deaths; in life these two men produced England's most successful public building of the 19th century.

ABOVE *The rebuilding of the Palace of Westminster was born of an ideal marriage of opposites in two architects: Sir Charles Barry and Augustus Welby Pugin. The Royal Gallery has a strongly panelled ceiling and patterns of Minton's encaustic tiles on the floor and Cole's flock wallpaper on the walls (all designed by Pugin), forming a frame for the two wide-screen frescoes by Daniel Maclise of 'The Death of Nelson' and 'The Meeting of Wellington and Blucher'.*

OPPOSITE *St Giles' Church at Cheadle, Staffordshire, 1845–8, is Pugin's most elaborate Roman Catholic parish church. Whereas externally his buildings are often very close to the medieval original, he let himself go internally, as in this Lady Chapel at Cheadle, in a maze of patterns in Minton's tiles, in Hardman's metalwork and stained glass, and in the stencilling of every inch of wall space with rhythms of crosses and crowns and abstract trellises.*

Mid-Victorian

THE WORLD of wind and water power survived from the 17th century, in windmills which still dotted the horizontal landscape of East Anglia, and in canals and river ports not yet covered in weeds. The age of coal and steam power and the use of iron was at its most prosperous in the pre-electrical era of the 1860s. Architecture was beginning to separate itself from civil engineering. Indeed, the Institute of Civil Engineers, with Thomas Telford as first President, had been founded in 1818, nearly twenty years before the Royal Institute of British Architects.

Civil engineers in those days regarded themselves as architects. Telford himself had worked as a mason under Sir William Chambers on Somerset House and later designed several churches and lodges. Robert Stephenson and the Brunels, father and son, both knew about the styles and orders of architecture. But no civil engineer was ever a Royal Academician, and perhaps one of the reasons why architects regarded themselves as artists was because of the connection with the Royal Academy. They felt they were above the building trade and above men who constructed tunnels and bridges and enormous greenhouses like the Crystal Palace. They tried to forget that Leonardo was also an engineer.

If you wanted to rise in your profession in the 1850s, you would join, if you were an architect, the Gothic side in the Battle of the Styles. True, there was still some good commercial work going for those who preferred the architecture of Greece and Rome and the Renaissance. The scholarly Sir Charles Cockerell was designing his handsome branches of the Bank of England in the provinces. Young Cuthbert Brodrick produced the Town Hall and a Corn Exchange in Leeds, and the Grand Hotel at Scarborough, in sumptuous Classic. But on the whole the style was considered a bit old-fashioned and stuffy. It went with merchants, banking, civic pomp and Nonconformity.

The influential men favoured Gothic. They believed with Pugin that the pointed arch was the sign of Christianity, and that Gothic was the only honest style. They did not want slavishly to copy the work of the Middle Ages – though this was better than copying pagan temples, and had been excellently done by R. C. Carpenter at Lancing (1855) and by the brothers Brandon in Gordon Square, London (1850–4). They wanted to go on from where the Middle Ages left off, and to bring the gospel to the slums of the new industrial cities.

This was a time when the big London architect counted for much. He was lord of his office and called his draughtsmen clerks. He terrified his customers, or 'clients' as he preferred to call them, with technical terms; he bullied the builders; the scaffold ladder had to be dusted if he found time to visit the site of one of his new works. This is a biased picture of the great Victorian London architect, who went by steam train all over England, visiting his jobs and acquiring new ones, but it is written to show the different relationship between builder and built – from that of a century earlier.

As mid-Victorian architects must be reckoned in terms of their personalities and styles, a few of the most prominent are listed here.

OPPOSITE *1875 was the year the Great Eastern Railway completed Liverpool Street Station, an extremely competent cathedral of steam designed by the company's engineer Edward Wilson. It has a strong division into nave, aisles, transepts and choir, with coupled columns and pierced spandrels; side walls are of red and yellow brick. The footbridge runs across in exactly the position one would expect to find the rood screen, and in place of the pulpit there are steps up to a first-floor buffet.*

RIGHT *The trains which carried the fruits of industry also extended the horizons of the craftsman, in that they brought to his door exotic materials. Butterfield's font at Ottery St Mary, Devon (1850–1), is resplendent with a kaleidoscope of brightly coloured marble chippings under a chunky cover; but in using only local Devonshire marble, Butterfield follows Ruskin's insistence on using appropriate materials.*

Sir Gilbert Scott (1810–77) was the son of a Buckinghamshire clergyman, and the grandson of Thomas Scott, the Calvinistic Bible commentator whose work greatly influenced the young Newman. Gilbert first took Gothic seriously when he read the works of Pugin.

First with a partner and then on his own, he built churches and public buildings, and restored most cathedrals and hundreds of churches and parsonage houses in the Gothic taste. For most of his life he considered the Decorated or middle-pointed style of Gothic to be perfection. This was when people believed that 'early' meant 'earnest and simple', e.g. Early English, and late meant 'debased', e.g. Perpendicular and flat-arched. Perfection was to be found in the middle.

Scott himself took the middle line in everything, he was neither too Low nor too High Church; he most ingeniously

OPPOSITE *In spite of Ruskin's propaganda Gothic remained the style of a minority of enthusiasts; Northern businessmen generally preferred the modernity and probity of the dignified Italianate classicism descended from Sir Charles Barry. Brodrick's Corn Exchange at Leeds has an elliptical shape which is exceedingly Baroque, solid and heavily rusticated outside, but incredibly spacious and defiant of gravity inside. The iron-framed roof, with its skylights flooding down clarity for the inspection of samples of grain, billows vertiginously upwards and outwards.*

ABOVE *Far from imitating the medieval, even the more sober Gothic Revivalists such as Sir Gilbert Scott interpreted it with great boldness. For the Albert Memorial in Kensington Gardens (designed and erected 1863–72) Scott took the idea of a canopied ciborium from the tiny jewelled caskets in cathedral treasuries; he then exploded the canopy to fifty times its expected size. Promontories of lively sculpture extend diagonally from the corners, and pink granite columns, mosaic tympana, and an elaborate metalwork spire complete the decorous ensemble.*

BELOW *The Midland Grand Hotel, at Sir Gilbert Scott's St Pancras station (1865–76), retains the original Axminster carpet on the giddily twisting staircase, with its double flights from alternate landings. The girders under the bridges are not concealed but are exploited with appropriately panelled and pierced ornament, composing with the railings into a Wagnerian idyll of metalwork.*

adapted the middle-pointed style to domestic use, as in Kelham Hall, Nottinghamshire (1858); the hotel of the Midland Railway terminus of St Pancras, with its grand stairs and magnificent skyline (1867), the Albert Memorial (1864), St Mary Abbots Church, Kensington (1869–72), Glasgow University (1864) and St Mary's Cathedral, Edinburgh (1874–9), are his most famous buildings. His inability to persuade Palmerston to let him do a Gothic Foreign Office for Whitehall is one of his few failures. He was well versed in building technique and his choice of stone and bricks is wise.

He had in his office, as articled pupils, most of the famous men of the next generation. He was breezy, bearded and genial, and in his forty-four years of practice accounted for nearly 800 buildings. His elder son, George Gilbert Scott Junior, was an architect of greater originality. This 'middle Scott' as he is called had a son, Sir Giles Gilbert Scott, who designed the red sandstone Cathedral of Liverpool and clothed Battersea Power Station in brick. The Scott family, in its branches of architecture, medicine, and theology, has probably had more influence in the last two centuries than any other family in England.

William Butterfield (1814–1900) was a remote High Anglican who looked like Mr Gladstone and was an uncompromising innovator, always building in the Gothic style 'going on from where the Middle Ages left off'. In London in 1849 he designed the brick church of All Saints, Margaret Street, which gives an immense effect of height, inside and out, in a small, confined site. It stands for strict Tractarian principles – one altar, and that the high altar, in the richest and most elaborate part of the church, the chancel; light coming from the west end so as to shine on books; the font and the altar representing the two sacraments essential to salvation, Baptism and Holy Communion, markedly emphasized.

Butterfield used bricks when he found the workmen in the district were used to this material. Since brick could not be

OPPOSITE *William Butterfield's obsession with polychromatic materials is seen in All Saints', Margaret Street (1849). On a narrow square site hemmed in by warehouses, he achieved a brilliantly compact layout, the short lofty church, largely lit from clerestory level, forming an open courtyard to the street, flanked by the clergy house and choir school and pinpointed by a high steeple recalling the Hanseatic cities of Northern Germany.*

ABOVE LEFT *The Gothic equivalent of the Grand Tour revealed to the Victorians the superior quality as structural systems, of the vaulted cathedrals of France and Spain. John Loughborough Pearson absorbed the structuralist logic of Viollet-de-Duc, which reached its high point in Pearson's work at the north London church of St Augustine, Kilburn (1870–80), with its system of vaulted galleries derived from the cathedral of Albi.*

ABOVE RIGHT *As the man who trained William Morris, Philip Webb, Norman Shaw and J. D. Sedding, George Edmund Street had every right to be portrayed on his monument in the Law Courts by H. H. Armstead as a medieval mastermason, orchestrating and conducting a complicated series of craft processes.*

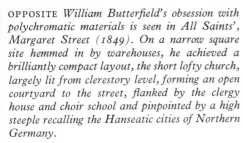

carved, he patterned his work with coloured bricks based on a principle of construction – strong bands at the base, where the walls had much to support, and the nearer the roof, as the walls grow thinner, the more elaborate the patterns. He delighted in making a continuous horizontal design and suddenly stopping it with a strong vertical. His most famous buildings are Rugby School Chapel (1875) and parish church, Keble College, Oxford (1870), and St Augustine's, Canterbury (1845). He had few pupils and was so reticent that he would not even come to receive the Gold Medal of the Royal Institute.

William Burges (1827–81) was the son of a lighthouse engineer. His buildings inside are substantial caverns of carving and colour – his churches are almost Oriental.

Famous examples are Cardiff Castle (1865), Castell Coch (1875), a re-created castle, Harrow School Speech Room (1877), the Tower House in Melbury Road, Kensington (1870–80), where he died in his own creation of Chaucer's Palace of Art, and two Yorkshire churches, Skelton and Studley Royal (1871), and St Finbar's Cathedral, Cork (1863). He also designed Trinity College, Hartford, Connecticutt (1874).

J. L. Pearson (1817–97) was another High Church or Tractarian architect, for this was a time when the Church of England took the lead in architecture at home and in the Empire. He specialized in vistas of stone-ribbed brick vaulting, and in giving an effect of height and endlessness to his interiors and diversity of skyline to his exteriors. His style was an Early English, adapted to brick. Towards the end of

his life he built some Classical work. He was withdrawn and gentle. His most famous buildings are St Peter's, Vauxhall, London (1869), St Augustine's, Kilburn (1870), Truro Cathedral (1879), Brisbane Cathedral, St Michael's, Croydon (1880), St Stephen's, Bournemouth (1881), St Alban's, Birmingham (1879).

James Brooks (1825–1901) built noble, big-boned brick churches, rising like battleships above two-storey houses in East London, such as St Columba's, Kingsland Road (1869), St Chad's, Haggerston, and St Michael's, Shoreditch, all about the same date. William White (1825–1900) was another highly original architect who did much work in Cornwall. His most famous London church is All Saints, Notting Hill (1855).

The most influential of the Tractarian church architects was George Edmund

Street (1824–81). He believed that an architect should perfect himself in all crafts, and he taught himself joinery, carpentry and blacksmith's work, and he could also paint and design stained glass. His work is always thoughtful and carefully detailed, and often so hard and sharp that it still looks quite new. He was the founder of the Arts and Crafts movement, and among his pupils were William Morris, Philip Webb and the brothers J. D. and Edmund Sedding.

His most famous works are the Law Courts in the Strand, London (1868 onwards), and the nave of Bristol Cathedral (1868–88), and his most beautiful are the simple stone mission churches he built in the diocese of Oxford. He always insisted that his pupils should travel and sketch, particularly in Northern France. On saints' days he gave his office the afternoon off. Norman Shaw was for a long while his chief draughtsman.

Besides these people in London there were provincial Gothic architects of influence and distinction, such as John Fowler of Louth, Lincolnshire, Pritchard and Seddon of Llandaff, Paley of Manchester, and Chatwin of Birmingham. There were also architects who specialized in the work of denominations, of which the most famous at this time were Scoles and Hansom for their Roman Catholic churches.

LEFT *Although the Victorians began by attempting literal imitations of medieval stained glass, William Morris and his group succeeded in breaking back to the true nature of the medieval craft. Sir Edward Burne-Jones' window in the Latin Chapel at Christ Church Cathedral, Oxford, made in 1859, has a vivid stream of strong colours finished off with a twist at the top by the sails of a boldly drawn ship.*

OPPOSITE *The Royal Courts of Justice in the Strand were Street's swansong; they were also the swansong of the dogmatic adherence to late-13th-century Gothic as the only pure model for 19th-century development. The cold proud vaulted concourse of grey stone runs back into the centre of the site from the Strand. This view is from the gallery which ingeniously unscrambles the changes of level on the steeply sloping site.*

Late Victorian and Edwardian

THE PEOPLE WHO PAID for buildings at the beginning of the age of electricity and the internal combustion engine were different from the mid-Victorians. There were a few rich manufacturers of armaments and very prosperous shopkeepers and bankers who could afford to build large private houses. And it is true also that architects, though not professional men, were accepted in the higher ranks of Society where people were still lucky enough not to have to work. It used to be said that the talented and versatile architect Norman Shaw (1831–1912) had especially large cuffs on his shirts, so that at dinner parties he could use them to sketch out an elevation of a house, thus securing a client in the guest sitting next to him. Whether this is true or not, Norman Shaw, who had been George Edmund Street's chief draughtsman, revolutionized English house building.

He used local materials and traditional methods of building when he designed country houses. His half-timber looked more genuine than that on the houses of architects before and after him. His walls were strong and thick. His chimneys were often external features which soared up the walls like buttresses. Inside, his houses had deep embrasures, vast Tudor fireplaces, subtle changes of level, and broad, stout stairs.

Friends from his days in Street's office, like William Morris and Philip Webb, designed the wallpaper, curtains and furniture. Rossetti and Madox Brown did the stained glass, William de Morgan tiled the fireplaces. He could design equally well in the style of Wren as that of the Tudors. He liked to make his buildings suit their setting and purpose.

Shaw was the inspiration of England's greatest contribution to the architecture of the Western world – 'the small house for artistic people of moderate income'. In 1878 he laid out in orchard land at Chiswick near London some winding streets of small Dutch-style houses which formed the garden suburb called Bedford Park. He used red brick, which had been unfashionable for a century, and white wooden balconies. A ballad of the time said of these houses:

> With red and blue and sagest green
>   Were walls and dado dyed,
> Friezes of Morris' there were seen
>   And oaken wainscot wide.
> Now he who loves aesthetic cheer
>   And does not mind the damp
> May come and read Rossetti here
>   By a Japanese-y lamp.

Shaw's career embodies the change of patronage. First he built large private country houses, but after Bedford Park he went in more for official buildings, such as Scotland Yard (1888), and buildings for banks and insurance companies and blocks of flats like Albert Hall Mansions (1879); in 1905 he designed the outside of the Piccadilly Hotel, with its great stone screen suggesting a cheerful banqueting house, and its arched front on Regent Street, which permanently upset the scale of Nash's stucco quadrant. He was High Church, collected clocks, and like Lutyens, who considered him even greater than Wren, he disguised his serious intentions in architecture behind a mask of wit.

From the 1880s onwards our towns spread outwards. The increase of suburban railways and the coming of electric tramcars spread them out still farther. Agricultural land was quite cheap, sandy soil was cheaper still; most people were only one generation removed from village life, and it was the aim of all who could afford it to have the equivalent of a house in the country, yet be near enough to the town to get to work in the day. Thus was Surrey populated with passable imitations of old farms, old cottages and small manor houses, Georgian or Tudor, by architects who had thoroughly learned under Scott, Street, and later under Shaw, the art of making a new house into a home instead of just a villa in a row.

The same thing happened in Cheshire, south of Manchester and Liverpool, and Worcestershire around Birmingham. A school of architects grew up versed in building in the style of the neighbouring country villages – Douglas in Chester, Bidlake and Bateman in Birmingham, Oatley in Bristol, the Tugwells in Bournemouth, Voysey, Lutyens, Baillie-Scott, Ernest Newton and Leonard Stokes round London and the South Coast and the West, and North in Bangor.

Described at the time as a 'magician's palace', the remote Northumberland mansion of Cragside was a characteristic mixture of advanced technology and Wagnerian sentiment in a spectacular Ruskinian landscape near Rothbury. The architect was the ingenious Richard Norman Shaw. Starting in 1870 from the existing hunting box (just visible left of centre), he created in stages over the next twenty years an exciting cliff-face 'village', combining monumentality on the outside of the garden front, with domesticity in the firelit interiors, including Morris glass and artistic furniture.

ABOVE *Under the influence of Continental Art Nouveau and the American experiments of H. H. Richardson, some of the Arts and Crafts artists of the 1890s, including W. J. Neatby, became more aggressive in their attitudes. In 1900–01, for the Bristol printing firm of Edward Everard, Neatby slapped onto an otherwise nondescript structure an unexpectedly bright-coloured façade of glazed tiling. Morris and Gutenberg, together with some sensual angels, are flanked by squashed turrets.*

OPPOSITE *The so-called Domestic Revival, by which William Morris's followers re-interpreted the traditional vernacular of the English cottage, had its supreme successes in the gradual evolution of the Garden City. The Garden City pioneers developed at Letchworth and Hampstead Garden Suburb complete communities, in which the cottage-with-garden was adapted for all classes of people. The northern end of Erskine Hill at Hampstead was designed in 1911 by Courtenay M. Crickmer.*

BELOW *C. F. A. Voysey invented a new style of Arts and Crafts cottage in which the wall surfaces were 'dematerialized' by being coated uniformly in soft stucco, with surprisingly synthetic-looking windows of yellow Bath stone and much white woodwork inside. He did not regard himself as anything but a Gothic Revivalist, and this recent picture of his own house, The Orchard at Chorleywood, Hertfordshire, built in 1897, shows the quiet absorption of it into the landscape which he himself must have hoped for.*

Houses by these men and their many associates are always a delight to enter, however small. The doors are of seasoned wood, the windows do not admit draughts, handles and hinges are practical and strong. Fireplaces draw, light from the garden outside comes into the house till late. They are not all perfect and some of them are quirky, but they have character. Liberal-minded and teetotal industrialists like the Levers, who built Port Sunlight in 1887, and the Cadburys, who built Bourneville outside Birmingham in 1889, tried to house their workers in what looked like old villages, and they gave them plenty of air, sometimes too much. In 1903 the first Garden City, Letchworth, was started, with Raymond Unwin and Barry Parker doing the layout and designing some of the houses. The idea was to have a self-supporting community with its own industries and market set down in a rural setting. Welwyn followed in 1919, but prettier than either of these places is Hampstead Garden Suburb, whose best houses are by Sir Edwin Lutyens, Barry Parker, Raymond Unwin and Baillie-Scott.

All these places, whether suburbs or garden cities, were built in reaction to grim blocks of artisans' dwellings and the treeless streets of back-to-back houses in industrial cities. They went with nut-eating, folk art and early socialism – 'work of each for weal of all' – and the ideals of Ruskin and William Morris. Thus you have two new sorts of houses born at the end of Queen Victoria's reign. There is the medium-sized house with its own tennis court and 'motor house', as garages were first called, and the cottage which does not look like a council house.

The first was derived by architects from mid-century designs for parsonage houses and the second was derived from lodges at the gates of mid-Victorian country houses.

The most original and delicate of these later house architects was Sir Edwin Lutyens. The most mannered and doctrinaire was C. F. A. Voysey, who liked to design everything in the house, from the doorscraper to the teaspoon. The most roman-

tic was M. H. Baillie-Scott, whose proudest boast it was that it had been said of him that he had built more houses that had done less harm to the English landscape than any other architect. He too, like Voysey, designed fabrics and wallpapers and cutlery and furniture.

The other side of the late Victorian and Edwardian architects was the public one, employed by ministries, local authorities and industries, the new patrons of architecture. The most prominent of these was Alfred Waterhouse (1830–1905) who designed Manchester Town Hall in the Gothic style (1868) – a clear plan on a triangular site, with the main rooms on the first floor approached by a broad double staircase. It was the aim of these architects of public buildings to state their purpose as soon as you entered, either a staircase or a corridor should lead you naturally to the chief room of the building. This was more often a town hall, a library, a museum or a council chamber than a chapel.

Other famous Waterhouse buildings were the Natural History Museum, South Kensington (1873), Eaton Hall, Cheshire (1867), and the Prudential Assurance Buildings, Holborn, London (1879 and later). He made great use of terra cotta for his exteriors, as it was washable. He was a practical North Countryman with drive and charm and more sensibility than he is credited with. He restored the old houses in Staple Inn, Holborn.

There were more sensitive men than Waterhouse in the public building business, and one of the best was T. E. Collcutt (1840–1924) who designed Wakefield Town Hall (1880), the Palace Theatre

(1891) and the Imperial Institute, South Kensington (1893), which has been destroyed (except for its tower) by London University. Collcutt devised his own version of the Renaissance style.

By the time King Edward came to the throne, town councils, banks and government offices preferred new buildings to look like the work of Sir Christopher Wren, only bigger. Some architects were very good at this sort of thing in a swaggering way, and none more than the now little regarded Sir Brumwell Thomas (1868–1948) who designed the City Hall at Belfast (1906) with a central dome like St Paul's and corner towers like the bell towers of that cathedral, and a lavish marble interior. He also designed the town halls of Woolwich (1908) and Stockport (1908). There was a master of Viennese baroque in King Edward's reign,

ABOVE *Alfred Waterhouse's career reached its peak with the Manchester Town Hall competition in 1867. It is in this building that his real virtues as an artist-architect are most apparent, particularly in the glorious sequence of vaulted reception spaces – from the many-pillared entrance hall, up the grand staircase to the lobby outside the Great Hall (with its Ford Madox Brown frescoes), and then up intricate spiral staircases at each side to the upper floors.*

Edwin Rickards, the friend of Arnold Bennett. With his partner Lanchester he designed the City Hall and Law Courts at Cardiff (1897), Deptford Town Hall (1902) and Central Hall, Westminster (1905). Another public architect in the Roman Classical style was Sir Edwin Cooper (1873–1942).

The most elegant of these Edwardian Imperial architects was the firm of Mewes and Davis, who designed the first steel-framed building in London, the Ritz Hotel (1900–06), and the Royal Automobile Club, Pall Mall (1908–11). These have a French look. Liverpool's Adelphi Hotel by Frank Atkinson is another fine building in the Edwardian Sumptuous Classic tradition. Not all these pre-1914 public buildings were Wrenish or even baroque. Henry T. Hare (1860–1921) in his County Offices, Stafford (1892), his Tudor Westminster College, Cambridge (1897), his Town Hall at Oxford (1897), Municipal Buildings in Crewe (1903) and University College, Bangor (1907), could produce a Gothic or Renaissance building carefully considered in every detail down to door handles and light fittings.

The two grandest achievements were ecclesiastical. One is the basilican Roman Catholic Cathedral at Westminster (1895) by J. F. Bentley (1839–1902). Bentley used red brick and bands of white Portland stone for his domed exterior, and his vast brick-vaulted interior has as its climax the high altar under a baldachin beyond the transept crossing. Bentley used electricity to light the church and treated the light bulbs as pearls suspended on flex from coronals and other devices specially designed to show them off. He accepted electricity as part of architecture as easily as civil engineers at the end of the 18th century accepted iron construction.

The other great achievement was the red-sandstone Anglican Cathedral at Liverpool (1904) by Sir Giles Gilbert Scott (1880–1960), a style which might be called late Gothic, freely treated. Scott owed much to his father's old friend G. F. Bodley (1827–1907), the church architect

OPPOSITE *The soap king W. H. Lever's garden suburb of Port Sunlight in Cheshire was begun in 1887. Its architecture and landscape are, in an almshousey way, remarkably generous, Lever himself being a pioneer of healthy house-planning; this three-sided courtyard, in the typical Cheshire mixture of brick and half-timber, was designed by his company architect, J. Lomax-Simpson, in 1913.*

whose churches at Hoar Cross, Staffordshire, and Clumber, Nottinghamshire,
Holy Trinity, Kensington Gore, London,
and St Augustine's, Pendlebury, prepare
one for the soaring, delicate Gothic of Sir
Giles's cathedral. Sir Giles was articled to
another great church architect, Temple
Moore (1856–1920), who designed St
Wilfred's, Harrogate, and All Saints',
Tooting Graveney, in a severe style of simplified Perpendicular Gothic which distinguished him from all others.

The days of the big names in architecture almost ceased after the First World
War.

LEFT *The Entente Cordiale of Edward VII's
trips to Biarritz, coinciding as it did with an
Indian summer of carefree wealth, made it natural
for Parisian influence to enthuse young Edwardian
architects. Arthur J. Davis really captured, in
interiors like the Ritz dining room (1903), the
wit of the best in Paris; but he subtly added to it
the English scale of domestic intimacy.*

ABOVE *Progressive architects in the 1890s were
fascinated by the Byzantine. The most influential
building in the style, Westminster Cathedral
(1895–1903), designed by J. F. Bentley, is a
masterpiece in striped brick and stone in an
intricate pattern of bonding, the domes being
all-brick in order to prove that the good craftsman
had no need of steel or concrete.*

MIDDLE *A generation after the romance of
Cragside, Norman Shaw turned to monumental
classicism, in his bright red rectangular palace of
Bryanston in Dorset. Built in 1890–4, Bryanston
is an amazingly grand conception, more like a
town hall than a private house and eminently
suited to its present function as a public school.*

BELOW *The Surrey gardener, Gertrude Jekyll,
with her architectural protégé Sir Edwin Lutyens,
succeeded in inventing a kind of landscape which
combined the 'wild garden' of the cottage with the
formal 17th-century type. One of the most perfect
of the Lutyens-Jekyll collaborations was The
Deanery Garden, at Sonning on the Thames,
designed in 1900–01 for the founder of* Country
Life, *Edward Hudson.*

After the Revivals

THE LOOK OF ENGLAND has been changed more by motor cars and lorries and power stations than ever it was changed in the past. Those of us who can remember when roads were unmetalled and hedges on main roads were white in summer with dust, and who can recall when only trees and telegraph wires crossed the sky, and the songs of different birds could be distinguished in the suburbs as well as the country, can appreciate how great and quick the change has been.

The change in architects is seen in their training. What Sir John Soane, that best and most influential trainer of architects, had to say about the duties of an architect is worth reading:

> The business of the Architect is to make the designs and estimates, to direct the works, and to measure and value the different parts; he is the intermediate agent between the employer whose honour and interest he is to study, and the mechanic, whose rights he is to defend. His position implies great trust; he is responsible for the mistakes, negligences, and ignorance of those he employs; and above all, he is to take care that the workmen's bills do not exceed his own estimates. If these are the duties of an architect, with what propriety can his situation, and that of the builder or the contractor, be united?

When practising architects, who took in clerks and articled them, were conscientious, as were most of the great Victorian architects, the young learned well; but some architects were not so conscientious, and the subject became wider and wider. Men did not have to design single houses, but whole groups of

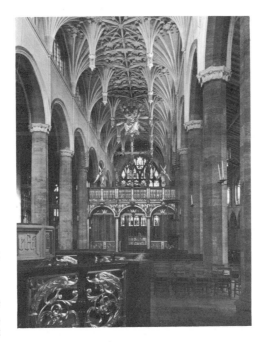

ABOVE *St Mary's, Wellingborough (1908–30) was Sir Ninian Comper's most complete achievement. Plain brown ironstone without, St Mary's is a glittering fantasy within, with an amazing lierne vault with pendants constructed of stucco almost as John Nash might have done. The rood screen and baldacchino are classical, the window tracery and stained glass Gothic.*

OPPOSITE *Even the unseen waves of radio cannot pass through solid earth; hence the Post Office's need for a telecommunications tower as much as 619 ft high, in order to have a clear passage over the heights of North London. The design by Eric Bedford, chief architect to the Ministry of Public Building and Works, had a stormy passage behind the scenes with the Royal Fine Art Commission, being modified again and again so that, like Wren's St Paul's, it completely changed its appearance several times. The result is an improbable triumph for the pragmatism of the committee system: a slender campanile surprisingly similar to one of Wren's in its disposition, with revolving restaurant in place of belfry.*

houses; they had to work not for private patrons only, but committees of warring councillors; by-laws increased; the power of local authorities was extended; the scope for individual design grew less and less. Schools of architects were founded in the last century and in this, and they increased in influence. Five years at an architectural school entitled you to put ARIBA after your name. A few years more and you could be an FRIBA if you wanted.

An architect registration bill was passed before the last war, whereby no one could call himself an architect without being accepted as qualified by the Registration Council. Certain great architects objected to this, notably Sir Edwin Lutyens (1869–1944) and another man of genius, the church architect Sir Ninian Comper (1864–1960), who continued to put 'architect, not registered' in his entry in *Who's Who*. He was knighted for the excellence of his buildings, of which the finest is St Mary's, Wellingborough (1908–31), despite this defiance after the Registration Act was passed.

The articled system never died out, but the influence of the schools, and with them schools of thought about architecture, greatly increased. Professor Reilly at the School of Architecture in Liverpool had great influence from 1914 onwards, and trained men who are now famous. The Architectural Association in London was equally influential. The tendency was to regard styles as superficial, and to despise the imitation of Georgian architecture, so that the word 'neo-Georgian' by the 1930s was an expression of contempt. The neo-Georgian school, on the other hand, produced some beautiful buildings, notably the Duchy of Cornwall Estate in Kennington, London, by Adshead and Ramsey (1913 onwards), which is in the late-Georgian style of South London adapted to modern use, and kept down to human scale.

In other places and by other architects, notably the then LCC and the Manchester Corporation, it proliferated into over-large suburbs of semi-detached brick cottages, in gardens of their own, which may have looked all right when one drove through in a motor car, and spacious in plan when seen from the air, but were lonely places to live in, far from shops and meeting-places and public transport. Becontree in Essex and Wythenshawe in Cheshire are notable examples.

There were also very distinguished practitioners of the neo-Georgian style, such as Smith and Brewer, who designed the National Museum of Wales in Cardiff, the old part of Heal's shop in Tottenham Court Road, London, and Ditton Place, Balcombe, Sussex, though these are all Edwardian buildings. Another famous neo-Georgian, who belongs to the days of articled clerks, is Vincent Harris, born in 1879, the designer of Manchester Public Library and the first new buildings for Exeter University, and what used to be Atkinson's Scent Shop in Bond Street, with its Gothic spirelet and chimes.

In the 1920s, Edwardian, even the Frenchified Edwardian which Sir Reginald Blomfield (1856–1942) employed in the Regent Street Quadrant and Piccadilly Circus, was regarded as rather vulgar. Decoration had to be restrained outside and in pastel shades inside. People looked to Scandinavia for inspiration. Sir Edward Maufe, born in 1883, the designer of Guildford Cathedral, several churches and the additions to Heal's shop, Louis de Soissons (1890–1962) at Welwyn, C. H. James (1893–1953) at Norwich, and Grey Wornum (1888–1957), who designed the new premises of the RIBA in Portland Place (1932–4), were the masters of the new restrained style springing from late Georgian and late Gothic after a visit to Scandinavia. They were practical and took great care over detail, as in the old tradition.

Meanwhile, in the world of builders as opposed to architects, fortunes were being made out of building two-storey semi-detached houses as close together as the by-laws would allow (sometimes closer), outside every big city and in almost every town and village. Clough Williams-Ellis, always ahead of his time, warned us against them, but in vain. The bow-windowed two-storey houses with half timber in the gables, which could be bought through a building society for so much a week down, increased as rapidly as the population, and transport by private motor car, bus and electric rail spread it over fields, so that people began to think there would be no country left anywhere in England, except for those areas where land was so unprofitable that it could safely be defined as 'national park'. The aim of the speculative builder

Courtenay Square's neat little houses, in Kennington, part of the Duchy of Cornwall Estate, are in a style of brown stock brick with trellis porches derived from the Regency. But in its urbane layout round a landscaped square this is a revival of the London vernacular which is far more than skin-deep, besides being the only distinguished example this century of royal patronage of architecture (the young Duke was later Edward VIII). The architects were Adshead and Ramsey.

OPPOSITE ABOVE *The engineer Sir Owen Williams' most prominent building is the* Daily Express *offices and printing house in Fleet Street, designed in 1931 in association with Ellis & Clarke. Black glass set in strips of chromium whizzes round corners outside, with a bold overhang to the leading bay. Inside is a fabulous Art Deco entrance hall, with wonderful rippling confections of metal and luminous glass suspended on the wide-span concrete frame.*

OPPOSITE BELOW When the Cathedrals Were White *was the title of one of Le Corbusier's books; and certainly in Middlesex the cathedrals were the great white factories. Wallis, Gilbert & Partners' Hoover factory of 1932–8 at Perivale on the A40 is described by Pevsner as 'perhaps the most offensive of the modernistic atrocities along this road of typical by-pass factories', which is another way of saying that it has one of the grandest of the great white fronts – a sort of Art Deco Wentworth Woodhouse – with whizzing window curves derived from Erich Mendelsohn's work in Germany, and splashes of primary colour from the Aztec or Mayan fashions at the 1925 Paris Exhibition.*

was not solidity or value for money, but an outward appearance that made it impossible for a visitor to mistake his products for council houses.

The chief employers of architects, now that the builders had got out of hand, were local authorities, and the chief influence on architects' minds by the 1930s, was the Frenchman Le Corbusier, whose book *Towards a New Architecture* had been translated by Frederick Etchells, FRIBA, the designer of London's first unashamedly modern building, Crawford's Advertising Agency (1930) alongside Holborn Underground Station. 'Modern' meant that you used the new materials, glass, concrete and steel, and displayed them proudly as the outside and sometimes even as the inside of the building. This had already been done skilfully by Maxwell Ayrton (who died in 1960) at the Wembley Exhibition of 1925. Even Norman Shaw had used concrete.

People in the 1930s were building for

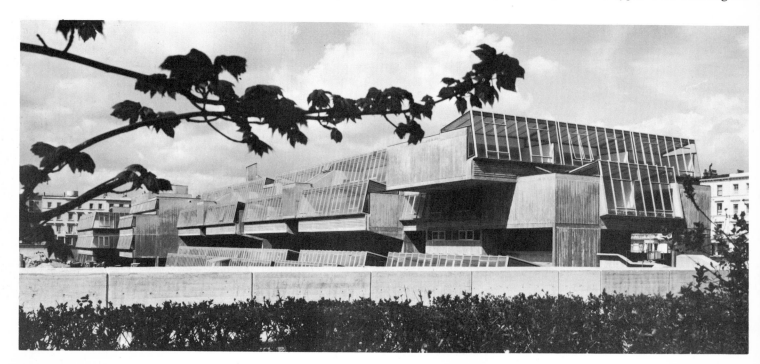

ABOVE *Pimlico Secondary School was completed in 1970 to the design of John Bancroft of the Inner London Education Authority. Vigorously planned around a broad internal 'street' at first-floor level, it projects outwards a jagged series of skylit classrooms, and, in spite of being lowered down a storey into the basement level of the demolished houses, there is no doubt it conflicts with everything around it.*

BELOW *St Paul's Cathedral Choir School (Leo de Syllas of Architects' Co-Partnership) has a highly sophisticated and delicate design which shows modern architecture already in its Mannerist phase, the curious narrow proportions being dictated partly by the upward-thrusting presence of St Paul's – and how much better it fits in than the perfunctory neo-Georgian next-door.*

OPPOSITE *Crawford's at No. 233 High Holborn commissioned in 1930 the first International Modern building in London, designed by Frederick Etchells and Herbert A. Welch. It is probably closest to the Berlin school, with its crisply chamfered corner and continuous window bands divided up by mullions of stainless steel.*

the future. The house must be 'a machine to live in', decoration was wicked and collected dust.

Preoccupation with the future caused distinguished architects like Gropius (1883–1969) and Erich Mendelsohn (1887–1953) to come over from Nazi Germany to England where they were welcomed by modern architects and the *Architectural Review*, the most forward-looking organ of its time in this country. Unfortunately the word 'modern' had come to be confused in the public mind with cubes and corner windows, so that cinemas were built in a style now called 'Odeon', which spread to housing estates and factories, and even to furniture. It may still be found lingering in garages and bus terminals.

After the Second World War public authorities and government departments, now the chief employers of architects, were concerned not to waste any land on the urban sprawl against which Clough Williams-Ellis had warned us in the 1930s. They thought that people must be housed in flats, particularly in areas which had either been bombed by the Germans or built by the Georgians. So tall blocks of flats were built without regard to the effect of gales and winds between them, and with little thought of the empty spaces that had to be created around them (so that lower floors might have daylight), and with no thought at all of the psychological effect on families with children who were forced to live in them. The architect became no longer an artist but a kind of public relations officer between local authorities and combines of developers, who employed him to give tone to their schemes for destroying old towns and creating new ones.

Here and there a few, a very few, private people were rich enough to employ an architect to build the sort of private house he and they wanted. Consideration of aesthetics was mostly regarded as a wicked luxury. Even today architects brought up in a generation whose romance is to be found in a future which does not exist, rather than the past,

find it hard to reconcile themselves to the fact, discovered by Sir Leslie Martin (born in 1908), that given a sufficiently large area in a city, it is more economical of land (as well as more practical and humane) to house people in squares not exceeding eight storeys high, rather than in point blocks over twenty storeys high.

The sad thing for architects is that their work has been taken over by civil engineers and the manufacturers of prefabricated units. I do not know what future beyond theorizing there is for an architect today. He is neither artist nor engineer, and yet he must be a bit of each, and a surveyor as well, and a sociologist and a politician and a mathematician. And of course a town planner. He is being asked to do too much, but with a little humility he may be able to do it.

We should wish him well, for he should be the only bar between us and the human anthill to which we may be reduced.

ABOVE *The ideal vision of gleaming white towers rising out of green parkland, which Le Corbusier had pictured in* La Cité Radieuse *(1931), at last came true in the London County Council's majestic Alton Estate at Roehampton (1952–8). In this view can be seen one of the Georgian survivals, Downshire House, now part of a college of further education, grouped starkly with tower flats and old people's bungalows. However brilliant as architectural sculpture, such blocks of flats have proved disastrous for family life.*

BELOW *Strongly modelled external walling was adopted by Andrew Renton in his office building for the Port of London Authority in St Katharine Dock, where he had to fit it in on a bomb-damaged site next to the magnificent Doric warehouses of 1825–8 by Telford and Hardwick. Renton's beautifully made concrete, with its exposed brown pebble aggregate, expresses in its rounded corners its nature as a poured material, yet possesses a classical nobility quite as impressive as that of any masonry. Inside by contrast the walls are almost all moveable partitions.*

OPPOSITE *Lt-Col. Richard Seifert has developed in conjunction with his partner H. G. Marsh a flashy and international style of crystalline concrete, seen at its most aggressive in the 380-ft tower at St Giles's Circus called Centrepoint, which stood empty for five years after its completion in 1967, making paper profits.*

Illustration Acknowledgments

The producers of this book would like to thank all those who have given permission for pictures to be reproduced here.

Page

1   Clarence Terrace, Regent's Park. Photo: Angelo Hornak

2–3   Capital in the crypt, Canterbury Cathedral. Photo: Jeremy Whitaker

4–5   Durham Cathedral towers. Photo: Margaret Harker

6–7   St Albans Cathedral tower. Photo: Margaret Harker

8   Maiden Castle. Photo: Edwin Smith

9   Avebury stone circle. Photo: Edwin Smith

10–11   *Old Sarum* by John Constable (1776–1837); water-colour. By courtesy of The Victoria and Albert Museum, London. Photo: Derrick Witty

12   *Above* Earls Barton church tower. Photo: Edwin Smith
Below Brixworth church. Photo: National Monuments Record

13   Crucifixion in Daglingworth church. Photo: A. F. Kersting

14   Church wall made of wooden logs at Greensted-juxta-Ongar. Photo: Ronald Clark

15   *Above* Saxon chapel, Bradford-on-Avon. Photo: A. F. Kersting
Below Saxon chapel, Bradwell-on-Sea. Photo: Michael Holford

16   Nave of Waltham Abbey. Photo: Edwin Smith

17   Saxon carvings on the doorway, Kilpeck church. Photo: National Monuments Record

Page

18   White Tower Chapel. Photo: A. F. Kersting

19   *Above* Nave of Durham Cathedral. Photo: A. F. Kersting
Below South Door, Barfreston church. Photo: A. F. Kersting

20   Castle Hedingham. Photo: Edwin Smith

21   *Above* Jew's House, Lincoln. Photo: A. F. Kersting
Middle Galilee Chapel, Durham Cathedral. Photo: Angelo Hornak
Below Hall of Oakham Castle. Photo: A. F. Kersting

22   Nave of St Albans Cathedral. Photo: Michael Holford

23   Stained glass in the west window, Canterbury Cathedral. Photo: Birkin Haward

24   Nave and south aisle, Lincoln Minster. Photo: Edwin Smith

25   Wells Cathedral. Photo: A. F. Kersting

26   *Pottergate, Lincoln* by Peter de Wint (1784–1849); water-colour. By courtesy of The Victoria and Albert Museum, London. Photo: Derrick Witty

27   *Above* Abbey Dore church. Photo: Edwin Smith
Below Restormel Castle. Photo: Department of the Environment

28   *Above* Stokesay Castle. Photo: Edwin Smith
Middle Choir triforium, Lincoln

Page

Minster. Photo: Edwin Smith
Below Capital in the south transept of Wells Cathedral. Photo: A. F. Kersting

29   Great Hall, Stokesay Castle. Photo: Edwin Smith

30   Nave of Westminster Abbey. Photo: A. F. Kersting

31   Great Coxwell tithe barn. Photo: A. F. Kersting

32   Chapter house roof, Wells Cathedral. Photo: A. F. Kersting

33   Capital in the chapter house, Southwell Minster. By permission of B. T. Batsford Ltd, London. Photo: National Monuments Record

34   Chapter house stairs, Wells Cathedral. Photo: Michael Holford

35   *Above* Stained glass in the south aisle of York Minster. Photo: Birkin Haward
Right Lady Chapel, Ely Cathedral. Photo: Michael Holford

36   Lichfield Cathedral. Photo: Edwin Smith

37   *Left* Strainer arches in the transept of Wells Cathedral. Photo: A. F. Kersting
Right Edward II's tomb, Gloucester Cathedral. Photo: Edwin Smith

38–9   Nave of Exeter Cathedral. Photo: Michael Holford

40   King's College Chapel roof, Cambridge. Photo: Edwin Smith

41   Cloisters, Gloucester Cathedral. Photo: Margaret Harker

Index

Page numbers in *italics* refer to captions.

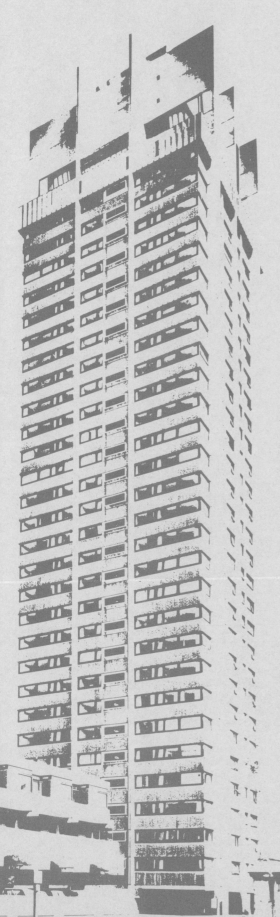